1-5□

SUNDAY TELEGRAPH

101
WAYS OF

INVESTING
& SAVING
MONEY

Published by the Telegraph Publications
Peterborough Court, At South Quay, 181 Marsh Wall,
London E14 9SR

First published September 1983
© *Sunday Telegraph* 1983
Third edition, updated, April 1985
Fourth edition, updated, April 1986
Fifth edition, updated, September 1987
ISBN 0 86367 202 7

The *Sunday Telegraph* cannot assume legal responsibility for the
accuracy of any particular statement in this work.

Typeset by Michael Weintroub Graphics Ltd, Kenton, Middlesex.
Printed in Great Britain by Biddles, Guildford.

SUNDAY TELEGRAPH

101 WAYS OF

INVESTING & SAVING MONEY

ALEX MURRAY

The easy way to make your savings soar

The Globe Investment Scheme is the simplest way to share in Globe's success. Judging by past performance, your Globe shares should do well – dividends have increased every year for the past 20 years, outstripping inflation by over 70%.

With a commission charge of 0.2%, the scheme is far cheaper than unit trusts, PEPs or buying through a stockbroker.

For the same ultra-low charges you can exchange any other shares you own for Globe shares.

You build up a shareholding in Globe in the way that suits you best. New investors can join the scheme for as little as £25 a month or a £250 lump sum, and you can stop making payments into the Scheme at any time.

The Scheme provides a very cost-effective and convenient way to invest without the need for frequent contacts with a stockbroker.

1987
£10,495
Average unit trust worth £6,663 after 10 years

1982
£5,185

1977
£1,000

*Over every one of the last 10 years Globe has outperformed the average unit trust and easily beaten building society and bank returns. Source AITC Statistics Service and Planned Savings Statistics to 30 June 1987.

THE WORLD'S LARGEST INVESTMENT TRUST

GLOBE INVESTMENT TRUST P.L.C.

To: Anne Rogers, Globe Group Services Limited, FREEPOST, Electra House, Temple Place, London WC2R 3BR. Telephone: 01-836 7766
Please send me further information on the Globe Share Investment Scheme.

101/87

Name ....

Address ....

.... Postcode ....

Preface

The extension of share ownership in Britain, the stable economy and the return of a Conservative government in the summer of 1987, pledged to the perpetuation of the 'enterprise culture', have meant an increasing interest by people from all walks of life in new ways to invest and save money. It is not only the stock market which is commanding greater attention from individuals these days; there are many new investment schemes being offered by building societies, banks, insurance companies and so on.

This book, first published in 1983, resulted from many inquiries by *Sunday Telegraph* readers who were unable to find elsewhere a comprehensive guide to the wide range of savings and investment opportunities available. But we have not focused simply on one or two areas – we have assembled details of a wide range of investments and savings, from bank accounts and stocks and shares to wine, horses and jewellery. There is much more besides – indeed, we have listed 101 ways of investing money productively.

In this latest edition, we have substantially updated the text to take account of tax changes and other developments in the financial markets and in the investment environment. I owe a large debt of gratitude to Matthew Bond who put a great deal of work into collating the new information, as well as to the many outside experts who provided advice. The book is not intended to be a complete reference book on each individual area but an easily understandable guide to the various options, noting the possible pitfalls and offering tips and useful addresses. I hope it will help to make our readers even more prosperous!

Alex Murray, City Editor, *Sunday Telegraph*
November 1987

CONTENTS

1 **INTRODUCTION**
- **1** What are the advantages of saving money, as opposed to investing it or spending it? — 11
- **2** Whose advice should I take? — 14
- **3** What are the tax implications of savings and investing? — 15
- **4** Do I pay tax on investment income? — 16
- **5** What is Capital Gains Tax? What are the rates of tax? Would I still pay CGT if my gains are not substantial? — 16
- **6** Are any assets exempt from Capital Gains Tax? — 17
- **7** What is Inheritance Tax? What are the rates of tax? When am I liable to pay it? — 19

2 **SAVING YOUR MONEY**
- **8** Should I put my money in the bank? — 22
- **9** How safe is the money I leave in the bank? — 23
- **10** Should I stick only to the clearing banks? — 24
- **11** What are the advantages of building societies? — 25
- **12** Is it worth taking out other regular savings schemes? — 26
- **13** Should I change my pension arrangements? What if I am self employed? — 27
- **14** Should I take out an annuity? — 28
- **15** Should I take out a life assurance policy? — 29

3 **NATIONAL SAVINGS**
- **16** What forms of National Savings are there? — 31
- **17** How can I open an account with the National Savings Bank? — 31
- **18** What are the advantages of National Savings Income Bonds? — 32
- **19** Should I buy ordinary National Savings Certificates? — 33
- **20** Are index-linked National Savings Certificates a good idea? — 34
- **21** Is it worth trying to win money on National Savings Premium Bonds? — 35

22 What are the advantages of Deposit Bonds? 35
23 Is it worth buying government stock through
        the National Savings Scheme Register? 36

4 **STOCKS AND SHARES**
24 What are the best ways of investing in stocks
        and shares? 38
25 How does the Stock Exchange work? 40
26 What procedures are involved? 41
27 What protection does an investor have against
        his or her broker running into trouble? 42
28 What are the costs of dealing? 42
29 Is it worth dealing within the account? 42
30 What is the traded option market? Is it worth
        investing in? 45
31 What is the Unlisted Securities Market?
        Does it offer the chance to make money? 46
32 Can I deal in stocks and shares outside the
        Stock Exchange? 47
33 Should I buy unit trusts? 47
34 Is it worth buying shares in an investment trust? 51

5 **OTHER FINANCIAL MATTERS**
35 Should I put money into the money market? 54
36 What are financial futures? How can I invest
        in them? 55
37 Can I make money out of commodity futures? 56
38 Should I become a member of Lloyd's of London? 61
39 Is it worth investing in the Euro-markets? 63
40 What is the best way to buy gold? 63
41 What about investing in diamonds? 66

6 **PROPERTY**
42 Should I invest in property? 68
43 What are the lending policies of the building
        societies? 69
44 What different types of mortgage are there? 70
45 What costs are involved in buying a house? 71
46 Is investing in a second home a good idea? 73
47 Is timesharing in the UK worth thinking about? 74
48 Is it worth investing in a farm? 74

49 Is it worth investing in forestry? 77

7 SMALL BUSINESS
50 What are the advantages of investing in small businesses? 79
51 If I want to start my own business, where can I get help? 81
52 What help do the banks provide? 82
53 Do I have to go just to the Government or to the banks if I want help? 83
54 If I want to start my own business, what are the pitfalls to avoid? 85
55 Can I invest in small businesses through a managed fund? 86

8 PUTTING MONEY ABROAD
56 What are the first things to consider? 87
57 When travelling abroad, is it best to buy currency before I go? 88
58 Can I make money by speculating in foreign currencies? 88
59 Should I buy property overseas? 89
60 Is it easy to transfer money abroad? 90
61 Can I open a foreign currency bank account? 90
62 Can I invest in overseas stock markets? 90
63 Is it advantageous, tax-wise, to work overseas? 94
64 If I do not wish to sell an asset before I return home, how can I reduce my CGT commitment? 95

9 ART, ANTIQUES AND OTHERS
65 When is the best time to buy art and antiques? 96
66 How do I choose what to buy? 96
67 Is it best to make a collection? 97
68 Is attribution important? 97
69 Where do I go for advice? 97
70 Are auction houses better than dealers? 98
71 How does an auction house work for me if I want to buy or sell? 98
72 Where do I keep the pieces once I have bought them? 99
73 What about insurance? 100

74 How do I find out how much a piece is worth?   100
75 Are rare books a worthwhile investment?   101
76 What are the best hedges against inflation?   102
77 What are the best bets outside furniture and paintings?   104
78 What about oil paintings, watercolours and prints?   104
79 Which precious stones are worth investing in?   105
80 Which period of antique jewellery is best to buy?   105
81 Are furs a good investment?   107
82 Are coins a worthwhile investment?   107
83 Where can I buy and sell them?   107
84 How can the coin market be affected?   107
85 Do medals make good investments?   108
86 What are the points to remember?   109
87 Do memorabilia have investment potential?   110
88 Are toys and trains a worthwhile investment?   110
89 Should I invest in firearms?   112
90 Are old cars a worthwhile investment?   113
91 Should I invest in old aircraft?   114
92 Is wine worth buying for investment?   115
93 Do I need to know about wine before I start and where can I find out about it?   115
94 Can I invest for other people?   116
95 Is it possible to share out the cost?   116
96 Should I collect stamps?   117
97 'D'ya wanna buy a horse?'   119
98 How do I buy a thoroughbred?   120
99 What about tax?   120
100 Can I save on a horse's running costs?   120

10 USEFUL ADDRESSES
101 Where do I go for more information?   122

1 INTRODUCTION

1   What are the advantages of saving money, as opposed to investing it or spending it?

By whatever route it comes to you, money is an asset worth preserving, unless you have so much of it that this does not matter – in which case you are one of a lucky and very small percentage of the population. If you are a salaried employee, you may be able to accumulate savings every month to spend at your leisure, either as a lump sum or in a system of regular payments. If you inherit money, it may come in the form of property or money – cash or investments. If you win the pools, make a killing on the stock market or are made redundant, you may suddenly find you have a large sum of money to take care of. Or if you are self-employed, your business may be earning you enough money to warrant careful planning of your financial opportunities, rather than simply letting the business take care of itself.

Whatever your circumstances, it is vital – though it is perhaps obvious to say so – that you decide for what purpose you need to plan ahead, if at all. If you have made all your plans already, then you may be looking only to safeguard your present standard of living. You may be prepared to consider some of the more speculative investments which may lose you all you put into them, or may double or triple your money. On the other hand, if you have a family or other dependants, and only a small amount to spare, you will need to make sure that your money is invested wisely.

Spending money on the needs of daily life is something that most people think of in different terms from investment and savings – and, of course, buying groceries, household equipment and so on, sees very little return, except in the standard of living which you have chosen. But even here, it is worth thinking about the longer term. Who would have thought, after all, that the Dinky toys which

11

so many parents bought their children in the 1950s and 1960s would have turned out to be a very promising investment (when properly preserved)? At the same time, the car you choose may, when looked after carefully, turn out to have some financial benefit to you rather than simply being a means of transport.

It goes without saying that if you decide to spend a windfall on the good life – drink, gambling and other expensive pleasures – then you have thrown caution to the winds, and can expect to have little left but memories. But if you would like to keep your money in some longer-lasting, more tangible form, then investing it or saving is preferable. Of course, there are moments when spending money, rather than investing or saving, makes financial sense in itself. For example, in the period of near-30% inflation in the mid-1970s average household goods were worth buying and storing in some quantity, because one knew that they would almost certainly be more expesive later. But such periods are difficult to predict. Anyway, this is really a form of investment akin to buying Chinese porcelain or good wine.

Perhaps the key distinction between spending money and investing it is time. Investing implies that whatever you have bought will be sold later, and some form of gain will be realised, while spending is mostly short-term. The distinction becomes somewhat blurred when you look at things like wine and furniture, which you may keep for many years and enjoy yourself. The key to investment is to buy something for the purpose of seeing your money grow, or to buy something cheaply now which will be more expensive in a few years.

Investing implies a preoccupation with capital growth (by buying an asset), while saving implies a concern for accumulating wealth (by lending your money to someone). In the former category, the field is wide open with opportunities from the stock market to coins and antiques, while the savings field is now enormous, comprising a rapidly growing range of services from banks, building societies, insurance companies, pension funds and so on. Saving implies preserving your capital, while investing implies taking a risk with it to gain an attractive reward.

There are many, many ways of using your money for financial purposes, but the first decision you have to make is whether to put emphasis on capital or on income. If you have a steady job, with a secure future and pension, you may be less concerned to bring in extra income, which can be realised whenever you need it. In this respect, it is important to remember that tying your money up in long-term plans (even including National Savings) or in property or fringe investments can be costly if you want to sell before the end of the allotted investment period or if you have to sell when the market for that particular investment is poor. Indeed, before you buy anything for investment, you should find out exactly how you can sell it again when you want to, and what the financial implications are if you do (like commissions or penalty clauses for early encashment). If, however, you have high income requirements, like a growing family or a large house, you will need to think about obtaining the best deal for a good return, though with less emphasis on capital growth.

The options today are very wide, and in this book we outline all of them. Before you enter any commitment, you should always remember to think through your own financial requirements. Normally, saving money means keeping it readily accessible and this may be attractive to you. But if you invest it, remember that there is usually a risk-reward connection: the higher the reward, the greater the risk. If you cannot afford to lose the money, do not be tempted to part with it.

● 2 Whose advice should I take?

There are many sources of financial advice, virtually none of them free. Since the passing of the Financial Services Act all are subject to far greater statutory control, designed primarily to give the small, non-professional investor protection against the sharp operator.

However, the Act has taken far longer than the Government had hoped it would and may well not be fully operational until the end of 1988.

Basically, what the Act says is that anyone involved in the investment business will have to be registered with one of the self-regulatory organisations (SROs), all of which in turn report to the Securities Investment Board (SIB), currently chaired by Sir Kenneth Berrill. Once registered the SRO will then approve the applicant or not if the individual or company is considered unsuitable.

These SROs include the Financial Intermediaries Managers and Brokers Regulatory Association (FIMBRA), the Investment Management Regulatory Organisation (IMRO), the Life Assurance and Unit Trust Regulatory Organisation (LAUTRO), the Association of Futures Brokers and Dealers (AFBD), and the new name for the Stock Exchange, the International Securities Regulatory Organisation (ISRO). From life assurance salesmen to City stockbrokers, everyone in the investment business will have to be a member of one of these organisations.

This system means that anyone with a complaint about the investment advice they have received from an SRO member can complain to the appropriate SRO, which will be running compensation schemes to recompense those with just grievances. It will actually be illegal to operate in investment without authorisation from the appropriate SRO.

Advisers will also have to decide, and inform clients of their decision, whether or not to offer best advice from a full range of financial products or to become a tied agent, selling products of just one company. Small firms who previously gave across-the-board advice are finding that the new Act makes it necessary for them to become tied agents and so the investor will lose out in the long term.

This one-sided effect does also mean that many professionals who used to advise clients informally – solicitors, accountants and so on – may now be more reluctant to carry on doing so. Indeed, some bank managers will be unable to offer prudent advice if the bank has opted for the tied agent option as some of them have – with the consequence that managers become little more than salesmen.

As advice from any quarter is likely to come expensive, it pays to stay informed. So the prudent investor should attempt to read at least some of the burgeoning amount of financial journalism. Both *The Daily Telegraph* on Saturdays and *The Sunday Telegraph* provide fairly comprehensive summaries of what is new in this financial field, as do radio programmes such as *Money Box* on BBC Radio 4.

The golden rule for investment in this new era of regulation must be 'shop around'.

3 What are the tax implications of saving and investing?

In every decision to do with your money you need to be aware of your tax position. Changing your finances could severely alter your tax liability, and it is your right to avoid paying tax wherever possible. In the table below we set out the main income tax rates with thresholds, and later on we give details of capital gains tax (CGT) inheritance tax (IHT) and other taxes. We also refer in subsequent sections to the specific tax consequences of certain actions and suggest ways in which tax liabilities can be minimised. Once again, it is best to take advice from those who know.

Personal tax rates for 1987/8

Rate %	Taxable income £	Tax £	Total income £	Total tax £
27 First	17,900	4,833	17,900	4,833
40 Next	2,500	1,000	20,400	5,833
45 Next	5,000	2,250	25,400	8,083
50 Next	7,900	3,950	33,300	12,033
55 Next	7,900	4,345	41,200	17,378
60 Balance	–	–	–	–

4 Do I pay any tax on investment income?

As from 1984/85, you will pay no surcharge on investment income. This surcharge was abolished in the March 1984 Budget as part of a wide-ranging reshaping of personal taxation. Investment income is taxed in the same way as other income, though it may be collected later.

5 What is Capital Gains Tax? What are the rates of tax? Would I still pay CGT if my gains are not substantial?

Capital Gains Tax (CGT) was introduced by the Finance Act 1965 and became effective on 6 April of that year.

Before there can be a charge to CGT there has to be a 'chargeable disposal' of a 'chargeable asset' by a 'chargeable person'. Put simply, when such a disposal is made, the gain realised is taxed at a flat rate charge of 30% (subject to the annual exemption and other reliefs mentioned below). An overall loss sustained, after taking into account gains in the same tax year, may be available to set against chargeable gains in future years, but it cannot be carried back. A 'chargeable disposal' can be any form of property in the widest sense but there are a number of specific exemptions, the major ones being listed on page 18-19.

You are a 'chargeable person' if, during a tax year, you are regarded as resident or ordinarily resident for UK tax purposes. (Special rules apply to those who are not domiciled in the UK and professional advice is essential on the complex subjects of residence and domicile.)

On death, although assets are revalued at that time, it is not an occasion of charge, and the property passing on death is deemed to be acquired by the personal representatives at the market value at that date.

There is an annual exemption for CGT which for 1987/88 is £6,600. This exemption is shared by a married couple. Additionally, there is indexation relief available which is intended to remove from taxation the profit resulting from the effects of inflation in the UK. Indexation relief is based upon increases in the Retail Price Index (RPI) as of March 1982. Since its introduction in the Finance Act 1982 it has been extended. One additional feature is that for disposals after 5 April 1985, if a loss is produced with the inclusion of indexation relief this will become an allowable loss.

If an asset was acquired before March 1982, you can elect (in writing) within two years after the tax year in which the disposal occurs to substitute the March 1982 valuation for original cost, but only for the purpose of calculating indexation relief (not asset cost).

An example of the CGT principles would be if the shares were acquired for, say, £10,000 and proceeds from the sale are £20,000 then there is an unindexed gain of £10,000 before annual exemption. Conversely, if the disposal proceeds were, say, £8,000 then there would be an unindexed loss of £2,000.

The changes in the Finance Act 1985 once again allow gains or losses to be realised by means of 'Bed and Breakfast' transactions in the same Stock Exchange account.

The due date for CGT is 1 December following the tax year of the disposal.

6   Are any assets exempt from CGT?

Gains arising on the disposal of certain assets, listed overleaf, are exempt; by the same token any loss arising on their disposal is not allowable for these purposes.

1 Betting and other winnings: Winnings from betting are not chargeable gains. Premium Bond winnings, etc., are also exempt.

2 Chattels: These are assets which are touchable ('tangible') and moveable. They are exempt if the disposal is for £3,000 or less (a special computation is necessary if the sum exceeds £3,000). This does not apply to currency (but see under 'Foreign currency' below). There are also special rules dealing with 'sets' of chattels.

3 Compensation for damages: This is exempt if received for personal or professional wrong or injury; if the damages, etc., relate to an asset, payment will constitute a disposal.

4 Dependent relative property: In addition to the main residence exemption, a property provided rent-free for a qualifying dependant may also be exempt. A married couple are restricted to only one dependent relative house exemption.

5 Foreign currency: This is exempt when disposed of providing it was acquired only for personal and family expenditure.

6 Government securities (Gilt-edged): These are completely exempt for all disposals made on or after 2 July 1986. (However, do take professional advice if you are contemplating selling a large holding with a significant amount of accrued income.) The exemption also applies to certain corporate bonds issued or acquired after 13 March 1984, and dealings in futures and traded options of gilts/qualifying corporate bonds.

7 Life assurance policies and deferred annuities: These are exempt when they are disposed of or realised by the original policyholder but not when they are disposed of or realised by another person who may have acquired them by subsequent purchase.

8 Medals and decorations: These are exempt unless acquired by purchase.

9 Motor cars: These are not chargeable assets unless they are of a type not commonly used as a private vehicle and unsuitable to be so used.

10 National Savings Certificates Premium Bonds, etc.: These and other government securities which are not transferable are exempt whenever they are acquired or disposed of.

11 Your home: Generally speaking, if your home is your only or main residence throughout your period of ownership, there will be no charge to CGT when you sell the property. This exemption extends to the building and in most cases up to one acre of land.

7 What is Inheritance Tax? What are the rates of tax? When am I liable to pay it?

Major changes were introduced in The Finance Act 1986 to replace capital transfer tax (CTT). The main substance of CTT legislation was retained but additional, rather complex rules which are largely based on the old Estate Duty provisions have been added. This new tax was called Inheritance Tax (IHT).

Some of the principal rules of IHT are as follows:

1 No initial charge on lifetime gifts between individuals and transfers into certain trusts.
2 Other lifetime transfers are taxable at half death rates.
3 Special provisions are in force for gifts of property which are subject to a reservation. These rules prevent a gift or transfer of value being considered as such where the donor retains an interest in the gift.

Lifetime transfers
There will be no charge to tax on lifetime gifts between individuals provided the gift is made more than seven years before the donor's death. Gifts into accumulation and maintenance trusts and into trusts for the disabled are similarly exempted; other transactions or events involving trusts, and gifts involving companies, remain subject to a lifetime charge. In line with the above, the ten-year cumulation period for chargeable transfers is reduced to seven years.

Gifts on or within seven years of death

Where someone dies within seven years of making a gift, that gift will be taxable in a similar way as transfers on or within three years of death have been chargeable to CTT in the past. The tax will continue to be charged on a cumulative basis, but over seven years as opposed to ten, while the estate at death will continue to be taxed as the top slice of the donor's cumulative transfers. Where a transfer is taxed both at the time of gift and on death (e.g. a gift into trust shortly before death) the lifetime tax will be credited against the tax due on death.

Exemptions and reliefs available under CTT, such as the spouse exemption and business property relief, will continue to be available in much the same way as before.

Gifts with reservation

Initially, such a gift is treated in the same way as any other lifetime gift. A charge may arise on the occasion of the gift, unless it is excluded property or the transfer is exempt or potentially exempt. The time when the gift will be reviewed, to see whether it is or was a gift with reservation, is at the time of the donor's death. If it can be shown that the gift ceased to be subject to a reservation at some time prior to the donor's death then the transfer will be treated as having been made when the reservation ceased.

Rates of tax

There is only one table of rates which corresponds to the previous CTT death rates. As for CTT, these rate bands are to be increased annually in line with inflation. However, those lifetime transfers which are classed as chargeable are taxed at one-half of the IHT rates.

The rates for chargeable transfers made on or within seven years of death are as follows and take account of the changes which occurred with The Finance Act 1987.

Chargeable band £	Rate %	Cumulative tax £
0 - 90,000	Nil	Nil
90,000 - 140,000	30	15,000
140,000 - 220,000	40	47,000
220,000 - 330,000	50	102,000
above 330,000	60	–

All transfers made within seven years of death are charged at the full table rates as at the date of death. But where the transfer took place more than three years before, the tax (not the value transferred) is tapered in accordance with the following scale.

Time between gift and death	% of full charge at death rates
4th year	80
5th year	60
6th year	30
7th year	20
More than 7 years	0

If tax is paid at the time of the gift or transfer and death occurs within seven years of this gift, tax is brought up to full death rates, with tapering relief if appropriate and credit is given for lifetime tax paid. However, no repayment is made if the credit exceeds the death liability of that particular transfer.

2 SAVING YOUR MONEY

● 8 Should I put my money in the bank?

Nowadays most of us have bank accounts, and if not a bank account, then a building society account. Between them, the banks and the building societies hold the vast majority of savings in the UK.

The basic principle of a bank is that it will make a profit for itself by borrowing money from one person and lending it to another. The major clearing banks have developed into vast organisations with many thousands of branches, each offering a wide range of services. But their bread and butter business is the taking of deposits, whether from the individual or from large corporations, and the lending of that money to someone else *at a profit* . For the individual the advantage of having a bank account is that he or she will be able to use the wide range of bank services on offer (and particularly the transmission of money by using cheque books and credit cards). There are two major types of accounts offered by the clearing banks. The first is the current account, which pays no interest, but which allows the individual to write cheques against his balance. The second is the seven-day deposit account which pays an interest rate broadly in line with market rates, but for which the individual has to give seven days' notice of withdrawal.

There are other options open to you, particularly among the more enterprising building societies. The payment of salary cheques by monthly direct credit is one obvious advantage of having a current account. But whether it is worth putting a substantial portion of your money into the seven-day deposit account depends very much on how competitive the bank's interest rate is. It goes without saying that it is not a good idea to hold any significant sum in a current account because it generally pays no interest. Individuals should be prepared to move their money between accounts, to get the best rate possible. Of course, you have to bear in mind your relationship with your bank manager in case you want to borrow money or use other bank services at some time. In this case you may decide to have available both a clearing bank current account and a seven-day deposit account, even though you may have other savings options. Generally speaking, the rates bank pay on seven-day deposit money are competitive with other options. Interest is paid after deduction of tax.

Apart from the simple current and deposit accounts, all the clearing banks have a wide range of savings schemes offering different benefits. It is impossible to list here all the schemes offered by the clearing banks let alone those of the trustee savings banks, the merchant banks and other banking institutions. But the clearers all provide the options of saving money for longer periods, thus earning higher interest rates, and of saving in regular instalments. The clearing banks are highly competitive with each other, but tend to offer the same range of services. You have to decide in what form you want to save your money, and whether or not to choose some of the more complicated schemes.

9　How safe is the money I leave in the bank?

Nothing in life is absolutely certain, but investing money in a major clearing bank must be as safe a risk as anything could be. Since 1979 the Bank of England has supervised the British banking system, under the Banking Act. Before being licensed to take deposits an institution must meet certain criteria demonstrating that its balance sheet is sound and its management 'fit and proper'.

In addition, the Banking Act introduced a deposit protection scheme which effectively protects 75% of the first £10,000 of any bank deposit. The scheme is financed by a contribution (0.01% of the sterling deposit base) from each banking institution on the list. It is hoped that this will be enough to deal with any crisis that the authorities can foresee. The events of autumn 1987 will have shown to a whole new generation of shareholders that the bank is a far safer place for their hard-won savings than the stock exchange.

10 Should I stick only to the clearing banks?

The clearing banks are the largest banking institutions and they include Barclays, Lloyds, National Westminster, Midland, Trustee Savings Bank and Royal Bank of Scotland, following its merger with Williams and Glyn in England and Wales, and Clydesdale Bank, Royal Bank of Scotland, Bank of Scotland and Trustee Savings Bank Scotland in Scotland. As explained above, the clearing banks have many advantages over the non-clearing banks in the range of financial services offered but there are several other kinds of banking institution (other than building societies which are dealt with below) which can offer the saver some interesting options.

1 The merchant banks: Many of the merchant banks, which developed this century as institutions specialising in servicing the needs of companies, now have a range of facilities for the individual. If you are worth several hundred thousand pounds or a million or more, you will find these merchant banks a perfect source of advice and investment opportunities, as they have well-qualified staff with a deep knowledge of financial markets. If you have less spare cash than that you will normally find that they will not go out of their way to encourage you to become a client. However, in the last couple of years some merchant banks, such as Schroders and Robert Fleming, have introduced special schemes to attract the small saver, including interest-bearing current accounts. Others, such as Hill Samuel, have regional offices in several cities, in which individual accounts are encouraged as much as corporate accounts. One disadvantage is that although some of these banks supply cheque books, these may not be recognised by shops and traders.

An advantage is that, in some cases, the interest rates they offer may be higher than other banks.

2 Foreign banks: In the last few years the number of foreign banks in Britain has doubled to well over 350. Although most of them are here for currency business, many also compete with British banks for sterling business. Not all are looking for individual customers but many of them are, such as the large American banks, i.e. Chase Manhattan, Citibank, Bank of America, and so on. Broadly speaking, the interest rates and the benefits of having an account with these banks will be similar to those offered by the British banks.

Many of these banks have their own individual schemes and some may not be interested in you unless you can make a substantial deposit. But with some of their services, such as mortgages, they can occasionally be more imaginative than their British counterparts and are often more aggressive in marketing their facilities. Almost all of these foreign banks are based in London although some have branches in major regional cities, such as Birmingham, Bristol and Manchester.

3 The Co-op Bank: This bank has grown out of the co-operative movement in this country, which has its roots in trade unionism and the Labour Party, although the links are now not as strong as they were. The Co-op Bank offers a wide range of personal banking services, though without the large bank network of the clearing banks. Nevertheless, it does offer a useful alternative.

4 The Girobank: This is a banking service operated throughout the Post Office and its 21,000 branches. It also offers the saver some simple savings schemes, at competitive interest rates. However, it does not have the same breadth of operations as the large banks.

11   What are the advantages of building societies?

At present there are around 11,250 branches of banks in England and Wales, with a further 1,500 in Scotland. The 'Big Four' London clearing banks alone hold just over £60 billion of sterling deposits including some £21 billion of current account money. By contrast the 123 members of the Building Societies Association (BSA) have 7,000 branches throughout the country and a total of some £120 billion of customer deposits.

The primary object of building socities is to provide finance for home ownership. Building societies are not run like banks and are subject to their own special building society legislation, rather than banking or company law. They are mutual bodies, effectively owned by their members who can vote at annual meetings on whatever matters of the society are put before them. The money for their mortgage lending (they lent £36 billion in 1986) comes from savers' deposits with the societies which are normally in the form of accounts where the money can be withdrawn with no notice like a current account in the bank. But, unlike banks' current accounts, building society accounts pay interest which is generally greater than that offered on bank deposit accounts. This explains why in the last 10 years there has been such a strong growth in societies' deposits.

In addition to the instant access account, most societies offer short notice and fixed term accounts with higher interest rates, also with tax deducted. In recent years, the societies have become much more aggressive in marketing their services and broadening the range of facilities they offer. Several have cash dispensers and some offer their own cheque books or have linked up with banks to provide this service.

The 1986 Building Societies Act gave societies a wide range of new powers – to lend unsecured for purposes other than housing, to build houses, and to offer a variety of services relating to house purchase and savings including estate agency, current accounts, insurance broking and pension schemes

One advantage that most building societies have over banks are opening hours. Most societies are open from 9 am to 5 pm on weekdays and at least part of the day on Saturday. By contrast, the banks close for business at 3.30 pm on a Friday with only a growing few opening on Saturday. A saver is well-advised to have an account at a building society in addition to a bank account so as to be able to take advantage of any new schemes either may introduce.

● 12 Is it worth taking out other regular savings schemes?

Apart from investing particular sums of money in one or more of the savings schemes which are available to the public, you would be well-advised to consider one of the long-term savings schemes on offer. These provide opportunities to put away money on a regular basis without reducing too greatly your regular income. And in some cases the Government offers tax advantages for the saver.

Wage earners contribute to Government welfare schemes through the regular contributions made to the National Insurance Scheme. Benefits they receive from the State include pensions, free medical care on the National Health Service and unemployment benefit if they are out of work. But many individuals find it useful to supplement their pension, for example by contributing to a company scheme (over which normally they have little control) or a self-employed pension scheme You would be well-advised to consider this.

13 Should I change my pension arrangements? What if I am self-employed? ●

An individual's pension is often his or her only asset though he or she may spend little time increasing it. But there are pitfalls to watch out for. Britain's pension fund industry is now worth a massive £80 billion and has grown swiftly. The principal anomaly in the pensions field is the inequitable treatment meted out by funds to 'early leavers', i.e. those who move jobs or are made redundant and leave much of their unclaimed benefits in the fund from which they are departing. One way out of the early leavers' dilemma has come from a number of insurance companies, who offer independant pension plans or 'buy-out' bonds under which a lump sum is transferred out of the pension fund into the company, and invested to produce either a pension or another lump sum on retirement. Insurance companies offering this include Crown Life, Equitable Life, Eagle Star and London and Manchester Assurance. Although guarantees are less than those under the deferred pension (which is related to the contributions made before leaving the firm), the scope for growth of the investments may more than make up the difference.

For the self-employed things are very different. To get more than your basic state pension (£61.30 for a married couple at the time of writing), self-employed people need to make their own arrangements and seek advice from professional advisers (such as Towry Law and Noble Lowndes). The advantages for the self-employed taking out an extra pension are far-reaching. Tax relief on contributions is given at the top rate of income tax paid, while investment in tax-free pension funds ensures a much greater potential growth than taxed investment. At retirement a tax-free lump sum is available and the pension is taxed as earned rather than unearned income although currently the tax treatment is the same.

There are two main types of pension plan for the self-employed: with-profits and unit-linked. Most popular are the with-profits contracts which provide guaranteed minimum benefits together with annual bonuses which will vary according to the profits from investment. Unit-linked plans can be more risky because their value fluctuates with the stock markets, but they do offer the potential for higher gains. The best approach is to spread contributions between both types of policy.

Choosing the right insurance company is the hardest part of the exercise and it can make a consierable difference to the results. A survey by the specialist *Planned Savings* magazine showed that the worst performing company paid around half as much pension as the best, from an equal start. A 65-year-old man retiring in 1982 who took out a with-profits pension policy in 1972 saving £500 a year would have got a pension of £1,724 per annum from the top-performing Equitable Life, but only £912 per annum from Gresham Life. Past performance is a good guide to the better companies, and some of the best-known City names recur year by year in the lists of top companies and fund managers. In the with-profits field, Equitable Life, Prudential, Norwich Union and Scottish Widows are prominent; while the newer unit-linked schemes are offered by M & G, Allied Dunbar, Vanbrugh and others. An independant insurance broker or consultant will advise you on the best choice. These contracts are also available for those employees who are not eligible for their company's own pension scheme.

As from April 1988 similar contracts will be available to everyone under the Government's proposals for personal pensions. Even those currently in a Company Pension Scheme will be able to opt for one as an alternative. But employees should carefully compare the benefits in their company schemes before deciding to leave it for another.

● 14   Should I take out an annuity?

An annuity is essentially a scheme whereby an individual receives annual payments after retirement age having invested a capital sum at some time before retirement. The 'purchased life' annuities operate so that where an individual invests some of his capital in an annuity, he receives the payments at a later date and part of the payment is treated as the return on his capital and so is not taxed. The remainder is taxable. The split between capital and income will depend on the individual's age at the date of purchasing the annuity.

It is also possible for an individual over 65 to borrow on the security of his house, and providing at least 90% of the loan is used to buy an annuity for himself (or jointly with his wife) he can obtain some tax relief on the interest paid. Details of such annuity schemes can be obtained from some life assurance companies or from investment advisers. These are worth considering for anyone concerned about their retirement prospects, though they need to be looked at in conjunction with other pension arrangements.

15 Should I take out a life assurance policy?

As from March 1984, new life assurance policies are not eligible for tax relief on the premiums paid. Previously, all premiums payable were eligible for 15% tax relief. The Chancellor did stipulate, however, that all existing policies taken out before March 1984 will continue to be eligible for such relief. The change only affects those policies taken out after 13 March 1984.

It still may be worthwhile, however, to take out a life assurance policy for the obvious advantages of providing cover against death, particularly for those with families, as well as offering a useful means of long-term savings. All the major insurance companies, including the Prudential, General Accident, Allied Dunbar, Scottish Widows, Standard Life etc., offer life policies. Do ask for a number of quotations, and study each carefully clarifying any queries you may have before making up your mind.

30

3 NATIONAL SAVINGS

16 What forms of National Savings are there?

The Government offers the public many forms of savings and investments – through the National Savings movement and through the financial markets. For example, government bonds and treasury bills can be bought in the City through stockbrokers and money market operators respectively. These are described in more detail in Chapter 4. The range of savings offered by the Government is wide, since in the last few years it has decided to finance a larger share of its borrowing needs through National Savings rather than mainly through the sale of Government Bonds to the markets. All the options available at the time of writing are described here. Further details are obtainable from most Post Offices, and the Department for National Savings, 375 Kensington High Street, London W14 8SD.

17 How can I open an account with the National Savings Bank?

There are two principal accounts: an ordinary account and an investment account. There are two interest rates in the ordinary account. The guaranteed rates for 1987 are 3% and 6%. To earn the higher interest rate, keep your account open for the whole of 1987 and then, for every whole month that your balance exceeds £500, you will earn 6% on the whole balance. For other months you will get 3%. The first £70 of interest a year is free of all UK income tax and CGT. Husbands and wives are each entitled to this £70 tax-free interest. Interest is earned on each pound held on deposit for complete calendar months. Money does not earn interest in the month of deposit or in the month in which it is withdrawn. You can open an ordinary account with £1, and the upper limit is normally

£10,000. You may withdraw up to £100 on demand at any Savings Bank Post Office during normal shopping hours, including Saturday mornings. Regular customers can exceed the withdrawal limits at a named Post Office. You can withdraw £250 cash at this chosen Post Office but to qualify for this you must have used an ordinary account there for at least six months. There are facilities for standing orders and payment of bills up to £250.

The Investment Account offers (at the time of writing) 10%. Interest is calculated on a daily basis and is earned on each whole pound for each day it is held on deposit. The interest rate varies according to general conditions in the financial markets. and the latest rate can be discovered by telephoning the 24-hour answering service on any of the following numbers.

South: London (01-605 9483/9484

North: Lytham St Annes (0253-723714)

Scotland: Glasgow (041-632 2766)

The upper limit on investment accounts is £100,000 with a £5 minimum. The interest is automatically credited to accounts on 31st December each year and is paid gross (i.e. without tax deducted at source).

To open either kind of account, you simply need to fill out an application form at a Post Office. Accounts can be opened for young children (although withdrawals are not normally allowed before the child is seven), by two or more people jointly, and for other parties in trust.

In many ways these accounts are similar to those available from the major high street banks; the disadvantage is that there is no cheque book, although the advantage is that the accounts are available throughout 20,000 Post Offices which have longer opening hours than banks.

18 What are the advantages of National Savings Income Bonds?

Income Bonds can be purchased by individuals or their children, by friendly or provident societies, by clubs and funds, by charities, by registered companies and by trustees. They offer monthly income payments at a competitive interest rate (currently 10.5% and access to capital at any time on three months notice. Your first investment must be at least £2,000. Larger purchases and additions to existing holdings are in multiples of £1,000. The maximum holding is

£100,000. Interest, which is paid in full without deduction of tax, is calculated on a day-to-day basis from the date your payment is received at the Bonds and Stock Office. Income is paid monthly on the 5th of each month. The first payment on a new bond is made on the next interest date after the bond has been held for six weeks.

Indexed-Income Bonds offer a unique monthly income scheme. Not only is the income guaranteed for a full 10 years but, as prices go up, your income is guaranteed to go up too. Like Income Bonds they pay a regular monthly income. Interest is calculated on a day-to-day basis and is paid on the 20th of each month. In the first year the income is paid at a guaranteed 'start rate' of 8%. On the first anniversary of the date of purchase the monthly income for the next year is increased to match the increase in prices as measured by the RPI in the previous year. This monthly income is guaranteed for the next year. It is then recalculated to match that year's inflation rate, and so on for the full ten years.

To buy either Income Bonds or Indexed-Income Bonds ask for a combined application/prospectus form at your nearest Post Office.

19   Should I buy ordinary National Savings Certificates?

National Savings Certificates offer tax-free capital gains over a short-term period, which is normally five years. Issues of certificates are normally held open for a limited period of several months, before being closed when a new issue, which takes account of changes in interest rates, is introduced. For example, the 33rd Issue of certificates, which is on offer from 1 May 1987, offers a return equivalent to a compound annual interest rate of 7% over the full five years. A £100 purchase after five years would have increased to £140.26.

An individual may hold up to £1,000 of the 33rd Issue although there are special facilities available for additional holdings of up to £5,000 for investors reinvesting their existing matured certificates, in addition to all other holdings of National Savings Certificates. (This maximum amount can vary with each issue.) The certificates can be bought in denominations of one, two, four, ten, twenty and forty units of £25 each. You can cash in your certificates at any time but the repayment value increases only at the end of the first year and at the end of each subsequent period of three months. The longer you hold them the more the value increases. Any saver or investor would be well advised to put some money into this simple tax-free form of investment.

Another way of buying savings certificates is to make regular monthly investments with Yearly Plan. By investing between £20 and £200 (in multiples of £5) a month by standing order for 12 months, investors will be issued with a Yearly Plan Certificate. The certificate needs to be held for another four years for the investor to obtain the maximum rate of return. The return on offer on the day the application is received is guaranteed over the five year period and all the interest is free of all UK income tax and CGT.

After 12 months' payments have been made, further certificates can be bought by simply continuing the monthly payments. Investors will be informed of the guaranteed return on their next certificate in good time for them to decide if they wish to continue with the scheme.

Yearly Plan is open to individuals aged seven and over, though applications can also be made on behalf of children under seven. Application forms are available from post offices. The completed form should be sent to the Savings Certificate Office.

● 20 Are index-linked National Savings Certificates a good idea?

Index-linked National Savings Certificates guarantee a return well above the rate of inflation for five full years. Not only is their purchase price fully protected against inflation, but they earn extra interest as well. Once you have held them for a full year their cash value will rise along with inflation (as measured by the RPI) over the previous 12 months plus extra interest for that year and each year thereafter until their fifth anniversary. Your earnings are inflation-proof and earn you the extra interest monthly from the date of purchase. So, if you buy on the 15th of any month your investment grows on the 15th of each following month. Repayments of these Certificates are free of all income tax and CGT.

Someone who bought earlier issues of index-linked Certificates in or after November 1982 and before October 1983 would be credited with a supplement of 0.2% of the purchase price for each calendar month up the the end of October 1983. This supplement will then be index-linked and will be paid when the Certificates are cashed, provided they have been held for at least a year. After five years the repayment value will increase by a bonus of 4% of the purchase price, which is in addition to the index-linked increase and the supplement. Other annual supplements of 2.4% (1983-84), 3% (1984-85) and 3% (1985-86) have been announced and at least two further supplements will follow. These will be announced early each summer.

Obviously, if the rate of inflation falls, these Certificates become less attractive compared with other savings opportunities, but it is certainly worthwhile if a saver has funds to spare putting at least some of his or her money in this inflation-proofed scheme. After all, no one knows what will happen to inflation in the years to come.

21 Is it worth trying to win money on National Savings Premium Bonds?

Premium Bonds enable savers to enter a draw for tax-free prizes whilst retaining the right to get their money back. The prizes are drawn by ERNIE (Electronic Random Number Indicator Equipment). About 170,000 prizes are paid each month. Prizes in the monthly draw range from a 'jackpot' of £250,000 down to £50. Each weekend there are prizes of £100,000, £50,000 and £25,000.

Bonds are sold in units of £1. The minimum purchase price is £10 and other purchases must be in multiples of £5 up to a maximum of £10,000 per person. Application forms are obtainable at most Post Offices and banks. Anyone over 16 can buy the Bonds and under 16s can have them bought by parents, guardians or grandparents. When you win a prize the Bonds and Stock office will write to you with the good news at the last address you gave them, and most daily newspapers publish the numbers of the high-value winning bonds. The money you invest in Premium Bonds pays no interest but you can get your money back at any time by filling out a withdrawal form at any Post Office.

22 What are the advantages of Deposit Bonds?

Deposit Bonds are designed for people who wish to invest lump sums at a premium rate of interest. They are best for money which can be left to grow for at least a year, though earlier payment is possible. Minimum purchase is £100, larger purchases may be made in multiples of £50 up to a maximum of £50,000, but this figure may be exceeded by interest credited.

Almost anyone can buy Deposit Bonds.

Interest is variable and is currently 10.5%. It is calculated on a daily basis and is added to the investment on the anniversary of purchase in full – without deduction of tax at source. As income tax is not deducted this makes Deposit Bonds particularly attractive to non-taxpayers. To buy these bonds ask for the combined application form and propsectus at your Post Office.

23 Is it worth buying government stock through the National Savings scheme register?

The quickest way to buy and sell government bonds, otherwise known as 'gilt-edged' stock, is through a stockbroker, who will act for you in the stock market. Alternatively, you could buy gilt-edged stock through a bank or other similar agent, but this will involve paying a commission, even though quite a small one (see question 28). There are commission charges on buying government bonds through the National Savings scheme register, but they tend to be smaller than those charged by stockbrokers. The charges are £1 for sums up to £250, and a further 50p for every additional £125 or part. On sales, the charge is 10p for every £10 up to £100, £1 for anything between £100 and £250, and an additional 50p for every extra £125 or part. The general rule is that gilts may be held by anyone and are not subject to CGT. Dividend payments are normally made every six months and are paid without deduction of tax. If you wish to buy gilts by this method, fill in the investment application form DNS400 (GS1) (available from Post Offices) for each stock you wish to buy, and send it in the green envelope DNS450 (GS3M) to the Bonds and Stock Office, Blackpool, Lancashire, with a cheque made out to 'National Savings'. Note that gilts purchased through a broker or bank cannot be sold through the National Savings Stock Register. This method of buying gilts may be useful if you have no connections with a stockbroker or bank and are not worried about buying at the best possible price. One disadvantage is that buying and selling orders can take a few days to complete because of postage delays and you cannot be sure of the exact price you will pay. But you may pay less commission.

4 STOCKS AND SHARES

● **24   What are the best ways of investing stocks and shares?**

For those who do not want to simply put their money in the bank or take advantage of the many savings schemes, investing in stocks and shares provides an opportunity either for long-term capital growth or for short-term gains, with the attendant possibility of loss as well as profit. Autumn 1987 spelled out just how real that attendant possibility is. Essentially, buying shares means buying a 'security' in a company, or a share in the equity, which is not redeemable or repayable in any form, but may carry a dividend each year depending on the company's performance. The idea is that a well-managed company will continue to increase its profits each year and that it will therefore be able to increase the dividend and, along with that, the value of its shares.

By and large a company which sets up in business will raise a certain amount of money by issuing shares and a larger amount by other means, including borrowing from the bank or in the form of a fixed-interest debt of a fixed maturity (i.e. a debt which will have to be repaid within a certain time, such as five or fifteen years). Because shares have no ultimate value, they can increase to astronomical levels if a company is doing well. The weeks following October 19 – Black Monday – saw the price of many companies' shares falling by 30-50%. They can also lose all their value if the company falls on hard times. Fixed-interest debt (such as bonds carrying an interest payment of, say, 10% a year) is repayable at a known time and thus its value can be more easily defined. The government bond market, for example, contains a vast amount of fixed interest bonds which have been issued by the government, and their value can be more or less fixed within certain boundaries because the money will ultimately be repaid at face value.

Larger companies have shares which are 'quoted' on the stock market, i.e. they are bought and sold every day in the market place and they are held by a wide range of investors. By far the best way of buying shares is through the stock market, through a stockbroking firm which will charge a commission every time you buy and sell. There are other ways of investing in companies, such as buying shares in private companies, but you can normally only do this through personal contact, and there is no guarantee that you will be able to sell the shares when you want to.

Stock Exchange companies are subject to rules and regulations laid down by the Exchange itself, thus they should be safer than non-quoted companies. But when the climate is gloomy for the market as a whole, or when particular troubles strike a company, the shares can fall sharply. Investors can make good money on the stock market, but they should be aware of the risks. If you want to invest directly in the stock market and have not done so before, contact either a stockbroker or a bank which can place the order for you. If you have any other general queries, contact the Stock Exchange direct.

Another way of investing in the stock market is through unit trusts or investment trusts, and we examine these methods in some detail later on. Unit trusts in particular offer the chance of spreading your risk (while limiting your possible gains or losses) and giving the key decisions to someone else, the manager of the individual trust. To find out which are the best trusts, read *The Daily Telegraph* (especially on Saturday) and the *Sunday Telegraph*, which are acknowledged as leaders among the national press covering this field. Telegraph Publications has recently published *Unit Trusts* by Tony Richards.

Personal Equity Plan: Since 1 January 1987 a UK resident has been permitted to invest £200 per month or up to £2,400 per annum in a scheme called a Personal Equity Plan or PEP for short, under which any capital gain or reinvested dividend will be entirely free of tax so long as the investments are held in the scheme for at least one calendar year. The plan must be managed by a member of one of a wide range of bodies, such as Stock Exchange members, licensed dealers in securities and a number of banks and other financial institutions. (Licensed dealers in securities will cease to exist at the end of 1987.)

● **25   How does the Stock Exchange work?**

According to the Exchange's own history, the market evolved in London during the seventeenth century from informal gatherings of stock and share dealers in the coffee houses around the Royal Exchange. In the nineteenth century other stock exchanges opened outside London, such as in Birmingham, Manchester, etc., and in 1965 these, together with London, formed a Federation of Stock Exchanges in Great Britain and Ireland. In 1973 they joined together to form the Stock Exchange.

Today the Stock Exchange has over 350 member firms, known as broker/dealers, who can act either as agents (buying and selling shares on behalf of institutional or private clients) or as principals (trading on their own account). Some firms also register as market-makers and so are committed to buy and sell shares at all times. In whatever capacity a member firm wishes to act, it is obliged to trade at the best possible price for its clients.

Competing marketmakers enter the prices at which they are willing to buy and sell shares on to the Stock Exchange Automated Quote system (SEAQ), from terminals in their own offices. When clients ask broker/dealers to buy or to sell shares, the brokers can instantly see the best price at which those shares are on offer. They can then telephone the marketmaker offering that price, and arrange the transaction.

About 6,900 securities are officially listed on the Stock Exchange of which 2,116 firms represent the equity capital of British companies, some of which are of quite modest size. The rest are a mixture of overseas securities, bonds, government and other public sector stocks.

There are now about eight and a half million individuals in the UK who own shares, and many more people have an indirect stake in the stock market through pension funds, insurance policies, unit and investment trusts. Savings in all these schemes are channelled through the Stock Exchange.

Investors should note that prices can move quickly according to economic or political developments, or announcements concerning the share in question. Investors are well-advised to keep an eye on their share prices by reading the financial press. Some speculative shares, such as Poseidon over a decade ago (which moved from several pence to £120 before falling back again), and, in 1982/83, Polly Peck and London and Liverpool Trust (which both soared before tumbling), can make money for the quick-footed. But the events of the third quarter of 1987 are perhaps the best example of how fickle the stock market can be. By all means have a go at these if you can afford it, but do not be too greedy. Remember those market maxims: 'It is never wrong to take a profit' and 'Always leave a little profit for the next man'.

26 What procedures are involved?

The market operates on a system of fortnightly accounts (or 10 working days). On the day that he deals for you, the broker will send you a contract note, which sets out the details of the transaction – the full title of the security involved, the amount bought and the price. The number of shares multiplied by the price gives the consideration on which broker's commission and transfer stamp duty is based. Until the share certificate is sent to you, which may take as long as six or eight weeks from the day of dealing, the contract note is evidence of ownership. Your contract note also includes the date by which you are due to pay your broker. In the case of government stock, it is usually the day after dealing. For company securities, it will normally be two or three weeks later. For overseas stock a variety of different times apply but the appropriate date will always be shown on the contract note.

Much of the paper work is speeded up by the Stock Exchange's computer system, known as TALISMAN, which keeps track of shares passing through the settlement process. If the company in question has announced a dividend to which you are entitled, but it has, because of the delay in arranging registration, gone to the previous owner of the shares, your broker will claim it on your behalf. To avoid the need for this, as far as possible, the Stock Exchange marks shares 'ex-dividend' some weeks before payment is due.

The procedure for selling is much the same as that for buying. Again, your broker will send you a contract note, but he will also enclose a transfer form for you to sign. This, together with your share certificate, must be returned to him in time for the settlement day shown on the contract note.

● **27 What protection does an investor have against his or her broker running into trouble?**

To protect investors, the Stock Exchange has set up a compensation fund to recompense clients who lose money on stock as a result of their broker defaulting. Payments from this fund are entirely a decision of the Stock Exchange Council, and, while it is rare for a claim to be refused, compensation is not automatic. The Council does not replace securities which have been misappropriated as compensation is always given in money form. Normally this represents the market value of the securities at the time of the default. Full details of this fund are obtainable from the Stock Exchange.

● **28 What are the costs of dealing?**

The system of 'fixed' commissions was abolished on 27 October 1986 under an agreement between the government and the Stock Exchange. Brokers are now allowed to charge as much (or as little) as they choose, so always ask what a broker's charge will be for your business and, if possible, compare this with two or three others before making up your mind.

In addition, transactions in securities are normally subject to government stamp duty, paid by the purchaser. Currently it stands at 0.5%. This stamp duty is payable on all equities, on stocks with an equity element, and corporate stocks, but it is not payable on government stocks.

● **29 Is it worth dealing within the account?**

If you both buy and sell an equity during the fortnightly accounting period, then you will have to pay stamp duty. You will normally only pay one commission charge to your broker instead of two. These concessions are possible because the stock in question has not officially been transferred to you. You can use this facility to deal in shares without actually paying for them, but it goes without saying that there can be substantial risks involved in this.

Traded Options

<u>THE</u> COURSE FOR THE PRIVATE INVESTOR

Traded options are the most exciting investment opportunity in the City today. Spectacular profits are regularly available — not just to the professionals, but to anyone with the expertise a specialist market demands.

The City Investment School offers an inexpensive but comprehensive home learning programme enabling you to deal successfully in the fastest-growing market in the London Stock Exchange.

- ★ **Twelve written lectures** prepared by experts and forwarded to you at weekly intervals
- ★ **Simulated trading** using our computerised link to the Stock Exchange, allowing you to gain invaluable practical experience — risk-free!
- ★ **Regular personal assessments** by experienced investment analysts
- ★ **An exclusive fortnightly Newsletter** and Stock Market update
- ★ **A software package** to boost your investment analysis
- ★ **Your own individual tutor** always available for consultation

For full details, ring 01-353 9365 or return the coupon below

— —

CITY INVESTMENT SCHOOL, 11 Bolt Court, Fleet Street, London EC4A 3DQ

Full name (Mr/Mrs/Ms) ....

Address ....

.................................Postcode.................................

Telephone ....

TT 30/7/98

30 What is the traded option market? Is it worth investing in it?

One way of investing in the stock market is through traded options. These give the investor the possibility of a much greater gain when a share price moves, but also of losing all his money quite easily. The idea of the option is to give the investor the right to buy or sell a certain amount of a particular share at an agreed price and within a stated period. If the option holder does not exercise his rights during the period of the option – because he decides it would not be in his interest to do so – then the option ceases to exist.

On the Stock Exchange, 'call options' give the holder the right to purchase shares in the underlying securities at an agreed price, known as the 'exercise price'. 'Put' options carry the right to sell shares. Each traded option contract normally represents an option of 1,000 shares of the underlying security. These contracts can then be bought and sold in the market independent of what is happening to the underlying share. For example, if an investor purchases an International Manufacturing July 300 contract at a price of 14p, this would give him the right to buy 1,000 shares in this company at 300p each at any time until the expiry date in July. Let us assume that the shares currently stand in the market at 290p. At some stage they rise to 319p – the options might then well move from the original 14p to 28p. In this way a 10% rise in the share price can be equivalent to a 100% rise in the option price. Of course, if the price of the share falls and stays well below 300p the option may become worthless.

People who sell options initially are known as 'option writers' and are entitled to receive the premium paid by the buyer on the first day of business. They commit themselves to delivering shares in the underlying security at the exercise price at the specified future date. The economics of writing an option are simple – the investor deposits share certificates with his broker to cover the number of shares represented by the contracts before or at the same time as he instructs him to write the options on his behalf. The repercussion of writing options can be devastating for those who get it wrong, as the case of the 23 year old who ended up owing close to £1 million pounds showed in 1987. As an alternative to depositing share certificates, there are certain types of collateral which may be put up, such as gilt-edged stock or cash.

Profits which arise from dealing in traded options are subject to CGT.

31 What is the Unlisted Securities Market? Does it offer the chance to make money?

In 1980, the Stock Exchange recognised the need for the addition of a junior section to the market, which would allow small companies to raise finance by issuing shares without going through the more stringent requirements that are involved in a full listing. The result is that companies which are traded on the Unlisted Securities Market (USM) are mostly smaller, younger and with less shares on the market than fully-listed stocks. They are therefore more speculative. Commissions on USM dealings are the same as other Stock Exchange share deals, and the procedures are the same.

There are over 500 companies traded on the USM, compared with 23 in 1980. Because the risks are generally greater on the USM, the shares stand at a higher rating (measured by the ratio of share price to the company's profit) than non-USM companies and can move sharply up. In the first half of 1983 a lot of money was made by investors on the USM as a result of these factors. There may well be more such opportunities ahead, but investors should be aware that the same factors which can exaggerate a price rise on the USM may lead to a sharper fall than normal.

On the 26 January 1987 the 'Third Market' was launched. It is designed to provide a disciplined market place for the securities of young, growing companies and those whose shares have previously been traded outside of the Stock Exchange. The market will be particularly useful to small companies who have not found it easy to raise equity capital through established sources.

The companies to be traded on the Third Market (13 at the moment) will in many cases be young and as such there will be relatively little information available on which to judge the quality of their management. However, these companies will pose a significantly more risky investment than those enterprises which are listed or quoted on the USM. Member firms, under the new Financial Services Act 1986, will be required to ensure that any particular transaction is suitable for the customer in question. It is suggested that you ask your broker for advice before dealing in any Third Market securities.

32 Can I deal in stocks and shares outside the Stock Exchange?

There are a few firms, mainly in the City of London, who deal in stocks and shares on an 'Over-The-Counter' (OTC) basis, i.e. they sell them to individuals and institutions much like consumer goods are sold across shop counters. But these are shares which, though technically issued by public companies, are for most purposes private, and thus are normally controlled by families or individuals. And, of course, they are not traded on the official stock market.

The oldest OTC market is that run by Granville and Co, which is both a licensed dealer in securities and a licensed deposit-taker. Its market works on the principle of matching buyers and sellers, and it does not itself take a position. Any licensed dealer in securities (licensed by the Department of Trade) will not be 'licensed' in the future but under the terms of the new Financial Securities Act 1986 they will have to be authorised from one of the five self-regulatory organisations set up. If you wish to buy stocks on this market, be sure you find out in some detail about the company whose shares you are buying. One advantage of investing in a new issue of shares on the OTC market is that the money you put in may qualify for tax relief under the Business Expansion Scheme (BES). This also applies to Stock Exchange issues on the Third Market.

33 Should I buy unit trusts?

One easy and very popular way for the small investor to put money into the stock market is by buying unit trusts. These provide a means of investing in shares without buying the shares themselves. They are particularly suitable for people who have neither the time nor the money nor perhaps the expertise, to undertake direct investment in equities successfully. On another level, they also provide a route into specialist and overseas markets. But investors should note the government health warning that unit trust advertisements have to carry: 'the price of units can move down as well as up'.

The concept on which unit trusts are based is extremely simple. Large numbers of investors pool their money in order to obtain a spread of stock market investments. The trust is divided into equal portions called units. The price of the units is calculated, usually every day, by the managers rather than being determined by supply and demand in the market. Two prices are quoted for unit trusts – the high (offer) price being the price the investor pays to buy units, and the low (bid) price being the one he will reserve for units to sell back to the managers. Unit trust managers are the only ones who are allowed to make a market in unit trust units. They must be prepared to buy units from the public and sell to them at any time.

The price of units is governed by the underlying securities of a fund. The price therefore fluctuates with movements of the market in which a fund is invested. Remember, the value of an investor holding in a unit trust can therefore go down as well as up and some unit trusts were hit very hard by the events of October 1987.

Initial and annual charges: The unit trust charging system consists of an initial charge and an annual management charge. The initial charge is included in the price at which managers will sell units to the public, and the annual charge is normally taken out of the income of the trust fund. The charge is subject to VAT at 15% but the initial charge is not. There is no upper limit on the charges that unit trust managers can levy on the unit holders, except that laid down in the trust deed. Although there is no agreed policy, the charges which have emerged since controls were removed are a 5% initial charge and a corresponding annual charge of 0.25% or 0.5%. Generally speaking, the annual charge on UK-investing trusts is lower than that levied on trusts investing in overseas or specialised markets.

Other charges: In order to avoid the need for quoting unit prices for awkward fractions of a penny, the managers are entitled to make a rounding charge of both buying and selling prices of not more than 1.25p or 1% whichever is the smaller, in addition to the initial and annual charges. A further cost to the unit holder is the 0.25% unit trust instrument duty levied by the Government, which is included in the offer price of units.

These charges together represent the whole of the additional cost a buyer of units has to bear, compared with the investors purchasing directly on the Stock Exchange (brokerage, contract and stamp duty are payable in both cases).

Control: Unit trusts are strictly controlled by the Department of Trade. A unit trust is set up by a trust deed, which is an agreement between the trustees and the managers of the fund. The trust deed covers the main aspects of the running of the trust and has to be approved by the DoT. The essential characteristics of the deed are that it lays down the rights and responsibilities of all concerned, the provisions enabling new members to join, the maximum charges that can be made by the managers for administrating the fund and the provision for calculating the buying and selling prices of units.

Investment instructions: Unit trust managers are allowed only to invest in securities quoted on a recognised stock exchange, although they may also hold up to 25% of their funds in companies traded on the USM of which 5% may be held in unlisted securities, whether USM or not. Certain other investment constraints are included in the trust deed to ensure that each fund has a sufficiently diversified spread of risk. The most important of these constraints is that no holding may be acquired which will result, at the time of purchase, in the trust holding more than 5% of its value in one investment. In practice, if an investment increases sufficiently in value after purchase it may well exceed the 5% limit, but as long as its value does not exceed 7.5% of the fund the trustees will not be too concerned. Another restriction on the managers is that each trust must not hold more than 10% of the issued share capital of any company. But with management groups running a whole range of trusts it is not inconceivable that between their trusts they may together hold more than 10% of the share capital of one particular company. Additionally, unit trusts are not permitted to invest directly in property.

The main purpose behind these constraints is to ensure that the investments held in a fund's portfolio are easily realisable. This in turn enables the managers to buy and sell units at any time.

Buying and selling units: Units can be bought either directly from the managers or through an agent such as a stockbroker, bank, solicitor or accountant. They can also be bought through any of the offers that frequently appear in newspapers. The buying price of units offered for sale through advertisement is usually fixed until the closing date for the offer specified by the managers. Units bought after the closing date are allocated at the offer price ruling on receipt of the investor's cheque. Units in new trusts are also often offered to the public at a small discount or with a special bonus. For example, one unit trust launched recently offered a bonus in the form of additional units, depending on the amount invested. If units

are bought through an agent, his commission normally comes out of the manager's initial service charge.

Units can be sold back to the managers of the trust by contacting the managers themselves or through an agent although when share prices are crashing there are always reports that unit trust managers can be difficult to get hold of. The price at which the managers will buy back units is controlled by the DoT. No commission is paid by the manager when units are sold back, so it could be cheaper to sell directly to the managers rather than through an agent.

The unit trust industry is vast, with many options open to the investor in the form of specialised and general investment. It is a simple and easy way to take advantage of rising stock market prices. Competition between the main management group of unit trusts is fierce and their performance is closely monitored by the financial press. Every investor with cash to spare would be advised to put some money into unit trusts, taking care to choose the more successful groups.

34   Is it worth buying shares in an investment trust?

Any investment trust is a limited liability company whose shares are bought and sold through the Stock Exchange in exactly the same way that shares are traded in other public companies. The assets of these trusts are shares in other listed stock market companies all around the world. Rather like unit trusts, investment trust portfolios are spread widely, something which the individual acting on his own would find difficult to achieve. When the first investment trust was formed over 100 years ago, it had as its stated purpose 'to provide the investor of moderate means the same advantages as the large capitalists in diminishing risks . . . by spreading investment over a number of stocks'. Investment trusts are exempt from tax on capital gains realised on their portfolio of investments. This allows the investor to defer any liability to tax on capital gains until he sells his shares. In addition, investment trusts – unlike some other popular investment forms, such as unit trusts – can borrow money to invest in assets, any appreciation of which benefits the ordinary shareholders. Investment trusts are not supposed to invest more than 15% of their assets in any one company.

In the last couple of years the investment trust industry has undergone significant change, with the managers of trusts being required to perform more actively and successfully than in the past.

By tradition, the shares of investment trusts tend to stand in the market place at a discount to the underlying value or 'asset value' of anything up to 30%. Recently the pressure on these trusts from return-conscious shareholders has led to concentration on particular and specialised fields of investment rather than on the general portfolio spreads of former times. In theory, an investor can buy £10 of shares for £7 or £8 by buying investment trusts, but unless the market changes its view of that particular trust (in which case the shares will rise strongly) the investor may only get £7 or £8 for the £10 of underlying share value when he sells. Of course, one hopes that the assets themselves will have increased in value so that the investor's money will have increased.

Investment trusts can only be bought through brokers and anyone considering investing in them should consult their broker or other adviser first.

DUNEDIN

JUST £30
A MONTH OR
£250 LUMP SUM

Only for the shrewdest of investors

Investment Trusts have sparkled in recent years, far outstripping the returns that have been available on deposit accounts with building societies or banks. Now monthly savings of as little as £30 or lump sums of £250 plus can be invested through the Dunedin Investment Trust Savings Plan. Dunedin offers a range of four investment trusts with exciting capital and/or income growth opportunities.
Key features are:
- No front-end charges
- Low cost buy and sell
- Immediate investment of lump sums
- Convenient and simple administration

The Edinburgh Investment Trust
for capital and income growth from an international portfolio

The Northern American Trust
for capital growth from an international portfolio

The First Scottish American Trust
for income growth without neglecting capital growth

Dundee and London Investment Trust
for capital and income growth from investment in small companies

DUNEDIN
FUND MANAGERS LTD
3 Charlotte Square, Edinburgh EH2 4DS
Telephone 031-225 4571

Post to: Dunedin Fund Managers Ltd
FREEPOST Edinburgh EH2 0BU
or Telephone 031-225 4571

Please send me details of the
Dunedin Investment Trust Savings Plan.

The booklet contains an application form.

Name _____

Address _____

_____

Telephone _____

ST 101/9.87

53

5 OTHER FINANCIAL MARKETS

● **35   Should I put money into the money markets?**

The London money market is a vast market without any central trading floor or official regulations (beyond those imposed by the Bank of England on some of the participants such as the banks and the discount houses). As its name implies, it deals in money, as opposed to dealing in stocks and shares or in commodities. In practice, money is defined as bank deposits or various short-term instruments such as Treasury Bills and Commercial Bills, which can easily be sold to raise cash or are redeemed anyway within a short period, i.e. 90 days. However, wholesale markets will become subject to regulation by the Bank of England this year. (See the joint Bank of England/HMS paper *Future negotiation of the wholesale markets in sterling, foreign exchange and bullion,* December 1986.)

The main users of the money markets are the professionals such as the banks, who have to balance their books each day and are thus constantly buying and selling large amounts of money from the discount houses, from other banks (often through money brokers) or from large corporations who themselves are doing the same thing. The professionals also take positions in the money markets to speculate on movements in interest rates, but normally they are simply covering their needs.

Individuals can also put money into the money markets, where the main advantage is that the interest rates paid are normally higher than those offered to small depositors by the banks but you do need to put a fairly substantial sum in. The clearing banks will be able to do this for you but normally will not do so for less than £25,000 at a time.

Money can be deposited for period of one day (known as 'overnight money'), seven days, two weeks, three months and longer periods. Interest rates are quoted on an annual basis and paid pro rata, i.e. if you deposit £25,000 for two weeks at 10% you will earn £96, or 1/26th of the annual rate. The bank's new regulations are designed to provide protection for investors in these wholesale markets, though it is assumed that most of these will be professionals rather than small investors.

Treasury Bills, which are issued once a week by the Government as part of its financing programme, can be bought in denominations from £5,000 upwards. They are generally issued for repayment in 91 days and pay their interest rate to the purchaser in the form of a discount on the price. These bills can be bought and sold at any time up to redemption. Local authority bonds and bills, with different maturities and different denominations are similarly available. Commercial bills (issued by companies as part of their trade financing) are available in much larger denominations, and certificates of deposit can also be dealt in from £50,000 upwards.

If you have enough spare resources or want to keep a large amount of money in liquid form for a while, then it is advantageous to use the money markets. But do consult your bank or other professional adviser, and do stick to the reputable names. Also make sure you find out what commissions or charges are being made on the lump sum – normally the banks do not charge commission but may take their turn by offering you a fraction of a percentage below the current interest rate. There are also a number of unit trusts available now with the object of investing in the money markets. Details of these can be obtained from the press or from your professional advisers. Remember that in the money markets, the return is almost always in the form of income rather than capital gain.

36 What are financial futures? How can I invest in them?

In the autumn of 1982 the London International Financial Futures Exchange (LIFFE) began operations a stone's throw from the Stock Exchange in the Royal Exchange Building. It brought to the City some of the market opportunities available in Chicago by allowing investors to take a view on the future movement of interest rates and currencies.

Essentially, a financial futures contract is an agreement to buy or to sell a standard quantity of a specific financial instrument at a predetermined future date and at a price agreed between the parties through verbal agreements on the floor of the Exchange. This is confirmed and guaranteed by the central clearing system. These contracts can then be bought and sold as the holders wish, which is broadly similar to the practice in the traded options market.

There are several contracts traded on LIFFE – including a short-term sterling deposit, a short-term Euro-market deposit, a 20-year gilt, and four currency contracts (sterling, Swiss franc, deutschmark and yen – all valued against the US dollar), options and a stock index contract.

This market adds to the abilities of large international investors such as the banks, and other financial institutions to deal around the clock, as there are already such markets operating on a different clock in Chicago and the Far East. In Britain the main investors tend to be the large corporations, banks and investing institutions who need to hedge their exposure to interest-rate and currency fluctuations.

Small investors can also participate as the amount of margin required for each contract is relatively small. Dealing costs are also relatively low, but small investors must know what they are doing in this expert and slightly esoteric field. If they get it right, money can be made. Conversely, if they get it wrong, it is possible to lose substantially more than their initial investment. Most banks, stockbrokers and other financial institutions will advise individuals on how they can deal in this market. The small investor is best served by staying either with options or, if he really wants to trade in futures, then the funds may be his safest access.

37 Can I make money out of commodity futures?

The volume of trade commodity has grown steadily over the years, largely due to the increase in world trade and in population. Essentially, the commodities market futures exist to service importers and exporters of raw materials, but they also allow the private investor to take a view on the movement in prices. Historically, the first official commodity exchange was set up in 1850 in Chicago, which was the centre of the rapidly growing American grain trade. Not long after, Liverpool established an exchange. A vital ingredient of this and all present commodity futures exchanges around the world is that they deal not only in the physical goods, which can be

The London International Financial Futures Exchange; Summary of Principal Contracts

	Three-month Eurodollar interest rate	Three-month Sterling interest rate	Twenty-year interest rate
Unit of trading	US$1,000,000	£250,000	A notional stock – 20 years maturity based on a long gilt – with coupon of 12 per cent £50,000 nominal value.
Contract standard	1 A three-month Eurodollar deposit facility arranged by the seller at one of a list of banks in London designated by the Exchange as deliverable names; or 2 A cash settlement at the buyer's option, based on the delivery settlement price ascertained and quoted by the Exchange.	1 A three-month Sterling deposit facility arranged by the seller at one of a list of banks in London designated by the Exchange as deliverable names; or 2 A cash settlement, at the buyer's option, based on the delivery settlement price ascertained and quoted by the Exchange.	1 Delivery may be made of any gilt with 15-25 years to maturity. Stocks with an optional redemption date will be considered to have an outstanding term to the first redemption date. 2 Stocks must be delivered in multiples of £50,000 nominal value. 3 No variable-rate index-linked, convertible or partly-paid gilts may be delivered. 4 Stocks are not deliverable within the period of three weeks and one day before the ex-dividend date. 5 Interest must be payable half-yearly.
Delivery months	SAME FOR ALL CONTRACTS i.e. March, June, September and December.		
Quotation	100,00 minus the annual rate of interest in basis points, i.e. one basis point is equivalent to 0.01 per cent.	100.00 minus the annual rate of interest in basis points, i.e. one basis point is equivalent to 0.01 per cent.	Price per £100 nominal value.
Minimum price movement	One basis point, i.e. 0.01 per cent (US$25).	One basis point, i.e. 0.01 per cent (£6.25).	£1/32 per £100 nominal value (£15.625).
Price limit*	100 basis points (US$2,500)	100 basis points (£625.00)	£2 per 100 nominal value (£1,000)
Initial margin**	US$1,000 which is the equivalent of a 0.4 per cent movement in interest rates. Straddle $750.	£500 which is the equivalent of a 0.8 per cent movement in interest rates. Straddle $250.	£1,500 which is 3 per cent of contract nominal value. Straddle £250.

Notes:
* Price limits do not apply to a delivery month during the four weeks up to and including the delivery day or, for the Gilt contract, the first delivery day.
No price limit applies during the last hour of each day's trading in each contract.

FT SE 100 Share Index	US Treasury Bond	Currencies			
		£ 25,000	DM 125,000	SW.FR 125,000	YEN 12,500,000
The new 100 share index, at £25 per full index point (£25,000).	US$100,000 face value notional US Treasury bond with 20 years maturity and 8 per cent coupon.				
A cash settlement based on the 'Exchange Delivery Settlement Price' (E.D.S.P.) ascertained by the Exchange.	1 Delivery may be made of any US Treasury bond maturing at least 15 years from the first delivery date in the contract month if not callable; if callable, the earliest call date must be at least 15 years from the first delivery data. 2 All bonds delivered against a contract must be of the same issue.	Currencies will be deliverable in the principal financial centres in the country of issue.			
The new 100 share index value divided by 10; taken to 2 decimal places.	Price per $100 face value.	Price in US$ per unit of currency.			
0.05 of a full quotation point (£12.50).	1/32 of a point ($31.25 per contract).	0.01 cents per £1 ($2.50)	0.01 cents per DM ($12.50)	0.01 cents per 1 SW.FR (£12.50)	0.01 cents per 100 YEN (£12.50)
100 ticks (£1,250).	64/32 ($2,000 per contract).	5 cents	1 cent (All equal to $1,250)	1 cent	1 cent
£1,500. Straddle £250.	$1,500 per contract.	$1,000 – Same for all contracts. Straddle $375.			

** On straddle positions, i.e. long and short simultaneously of different months in the same contract, where neither the contract months is 'spot', the intial margin of each pair of contracts is at the reduced rate shown.

bought and sold for immediate delivery, but in futures contracts. (Indeed the market is now known as the futures market.)

The contracts, which form a commitment to buy or to sell a certain amount of goods in a certain time, can themselves be traded on the market place. The main users of the commodity markets are producers (such as the Third World countries rich in minerals and crops), merchants (who buy and sell these commodities) and consumers (such as the manufacturing companies, who produce finished goods, e.g. cars, tinned foods and so on). One feature of commodities futures trading is the ability to trade on margin, in other words one only has to deposit 10% of the contract's value, which is the maximum; often these deposits or margins are much less than that. To take a position in these futures markets, whether for hedging purposes or for profit, usually involves opening an account with a commodity broker, who executes the order on the relevant commodity exchange. The client is normally then sent a contract detailing the quantity, delivery date, and price at which the commodity has been bought or sold. From that moment the client has an open position which – unless he wants to take possession of the physical commodity – must be closed later. If the price moves up, the client will make a profit, in which case he can sell and receive a cheque with commission deducted. If the price moves against the client then the opening position will be showing a loss. Normally, if this opening position's loss has eroded more than half of the original 10% deposit, it is likely that the broker will request that either the client closes the position (thus eliminating the possibility of any further loss) or that he send further funds to maintain the original 10% deposit. This is known as a 'margin call'.

There are two principle commodity exchanges in London – the London Metal Exchange (Plantation House, Fenchurch Street, London EC3) which deals in lead, zinc, copper, aluminium, nickel, silver and other materials, and the London Futures and Options Exchange in St Catherine's Dock which deals in soft commodities such as sugar, coffee, cocoa, rubber and so on. In addition, there are markets in grain, potatoes and petroleum. But if you deal in Britain through an established firm of brokers you will be able to deal on many other international commodity exchanges, thereby taking advantage of wider price opportunities.

Commodity price movements can be marked, and they depend a great deal on world economic conditions and as many unpredictable factors such as the weather, which can seriously affect crops, also strikes or political upheavals, which can interrupt supplies. Sometimes particular buyers enter the market to try and influence price movements.

Tin prices were supported by the workings of the International Tin Agreement (ITA) and specifically by the operation of the butter stock manager who was, in effect, buying up a considerable world surplus of tin. Late in 1985, the butter stock manager ran out of funds. The membership of the ITA refused to advance any further money and the butter stock manager abruptly withdrew from the market. Tin prices collapsed forcing a halt to tin futures trading and, subsequently, litigation between various interested parties including LME and the British Government. This is an exception but it does demonstrate that a monopoly buyer (or seller) can strongly influence a commodity market in the short and medium term. Nevertheless, all attempts to corner markets, even by inter-government agencies, have proved unsuccessful in the long run and price will always respond to the laws of supply and demand. However, if you wish to take a position in any futures market, it is always worth doing research on the state of the world in the under-lying commodity to find out what the present and predicted influences are on the price direction.

One important point to remember is that, following legislative changes, all UK futures exchanges have to be licensed by the Government. Moreover, the industry is now regulated by the Association of Futures Brokers and Dealers (AFBD) set up by the Government. Investors in the futures markets should trade only through a member of the AFBD and only on a recognised exchange. As with some other investments, the futures market offers a significant reward but with a high risk element.

Futures contracts

Exchange minimum daily limit	Commodity	Trading months
London Futures and Options Exchange ('London Fox')	Sugar No. 5-white	Mar/May/Aug/Oct/Dec
	Sugar No. 6-raw	Mar/May/Aug/Oct/Dec
	Coffee	Jan/Mar/May/July/Sept/Nov
	Cocoa	Mar/May/July/Sept/Dec
International Petroleum Exchange	Gas oil	All months
	Crude oil (Brent blend)	All months
	Heavy fuel oil	All months
Baltic International Exchange	Dry cargo freight futures	Apr/July/Oct/Jan
	Minimum price 1 point	Daily limit No limit
Agricultural Futures Exchange	Soya bean meal	Feb/Apr/Jun/Aug/Oct/Dec
London Grain Futures Market	1 Wheat	Jan/Mar/May
	2 Barley	Sept/Nov
London Potato Futures Market	Potatoes	Feb/Mar/Apr/May/Nov
	Early potatoes	July/Aug

London Meat Futures Market	Pig meat	All months
	Live pigs	All months
	Beef	All months
London Metal Exchange	Aluminium high Grade (in $)	
	Silver	Cash – 3 months
	Copper Wirebars	Cash – 3 months
	Lead	Cash – 3 months
	Zinc	Cash – 3 months
	Aluminium	Cash – 3 months
	Nickel	Cash – 3 months

Note: The table is reproduced by courtesy of GNI.

38   Should I become a member of Lloyd's of London?

Lloyd's of London is an insurance market in which insurance policies are placed with 31,00 individual members grouped in almost 400 syndicates. Each syndicate is managed by an under-writing agent who sits at his box on the floor of Lloyd's and accepts business on behalf of his members. Each syndicate member is individually liable to the full extent of his private means for his own share of risks accepted. There are four principal markets at Lloyd's: Marine, which carries every kind of shipping and marine business; Aviation; Motor, which covers more than one in five British motorists; and Non-marine, including earthquakes, burglaries and so on. All business is brought to Lloyd's by some 272 authorised firms of Lloyd's brokers who are not restricted to dealing with Lloyd's underwriters but may place business with the large insurance companies (such as the Prudential and Commercial Union) as well.

Those wishing to become members (known as 'Names') of Lloyd's must have the support of two existing underwriting members, one of whom must be a director or partner of his proposed managing agent. The candidates, who may be male or female, of any nationality, go before a committee for an interview and if approved their applications are considered at a full committee meeting.

The elected member places his or her entrance fee and lodges certain deposits with the Corporation of Lloyd's. These are held under trust deeds, and they are sold to meet underwriting liabilities. Accounts at Lloyd's are run on a three yearly basis, i.e. the account for year one is not closed until the end of the third year and then only as long as profits may be released. A new member must

61

therefore wait three years for profits on his first year's underwriting. The requirements listed below are applicable to new names elected to begin underwriting from January 1988.

1988 Membership Requirements
Applicable to all Names from 1.1.1988

Category	Means (£10,000 incs)	Gross premium underwriting limit maximum (£25,000 incs)	Deposit as % of GPUL†	Minimum deposit
		£		£
Lloyd's Names	Nominal	30,000	40	12,000
		50,000		20,000
		75,000		30,000
Lloyd's & Connected & Associated Names* Resident & Domiciled in UK	£30,000 (Minimum) To £70,000 (Maximum)	175,000	30	22,500
Connected & Associated Names* Resident or Domiciled Outside UK	£30,000 (Minimum) To £70,000 (Maximum)	175,000	40	30,000
Members Resident and Domiciled in UK	£100,000 (Minimum) To £520,000 (Maximum)	1,300,000	20	20,000
Members Resident or Domiciled Outside UK	£100,000 (Minimum) To £520,000 (Maximum)	1,300,000	28	28,000

* Includes Names on reduced Means.
† Gross Premium Underwriting Limit not to exceed 2.5 times Means shown.

If you have enough resources to become a member of Lloyd's, it can provide you with a useful additional source of income. After all, you will be receiving investment income and capital appreciation from the money you have pledged to the syndicate anyway. The amount of money the syndicate will pay you from its profits will vary according to the experience and skill of the underwriter. In a good year the cheque you receive may be many thousands of pounds, in a bad year it will be less. And remember that if you are unlucky you could end up having to write a cheque to cover the syndicate's loss if major troubles emerge.

You are also technically liable for your entire possessions. However, experience over the last century has for the most part been favourable and profitable for the members – which has made Lloyd's such a large and successful insurance market.

39   Is it worth investing in the Euro-markets?

Eurobonds are international bonds issued by various companies and governments to raise money. Unless you are familiar with the intricacies of the bond markets it is not worth contemplating investing in them. Like other bonds, Eurobonds are issued for a specified length of time and pay a particular rate of interest.

The Eurobond market is a vast and largely unregulated market, and is dominated by the professional dealing houses of several countries. It does offer the investor the chance to put money into other currencies and occasionally offers opportunities not available in the domestic market (particularly the practice of issuing zero coupon bonds which offer all their returns in the form of capital gains without income) which is attractive to many investors for tax purposes. Most major firms of stockbrokers or banks in Britain should be able to advise you on how to invest in the Eurobonds market.

40   What is the best way to buy gold?

Gold is an extremely rare and virtually useless commodity. Yet for over 6,000 years civilised people have fought, cheated, lied, slaved and died for it, but most of all they have hoarded it. Yet if all the 90,000 tonnes of gold ever mined were put together they would only form a cube measuring 19 cubic yards. About half of the gold coming to the market each year (including 'scrap') goes into jewellery while official coins such as British sovereigns, the new Britannia coin, the American eagle, Australian nugget and the Canadian maple leaf take between 10% to 15%.

Contrary to the popular belief that gold must be a good investment, its price varies wildly. During the 1970s, the price rose by 44% in real terms, but that sort of performance has not been maintained. The price touched $840 an ounce early in 1980, but fell to $300 an ounce in June 1982. By mid-1987 it was standing some $150 better than its 1982 level.

For the private investor there are two sensible possibilities for investment: gold coins and gold shares – although the latter can move up and down even faster than the gold price. The problem with buying gold metal in bulk, whether ingots or coins, is that if delivery is taken in the UK the sale is subject to VAT at 15%. Most of the gold dealing companies run schemes whereby you can take delivery of the gold in one of the off-shore countries, such as the Channel Islands or Gibraltar, where no VAT is charged.

There are a growing number of gold coins to choose from, some trade at a premium to the gold price and some, like the politically out of favour krugerrand, sell at a slight discount.

South African krugerrands
From the early/mid 1970s until recently, the krugerrand was the most widely circulated bullion coin in the world. The coin was made from 22 carat gold and contained exactly 1 ounce of fine gold. In 1980, three smaller krugerrands were introduced, containing 0.5 ounce, 0.25 ounce and 0.10 ounce.

The krugerrand has suffered dramatically from political attitudes towards South Africa and production of the coins has now ceased. Although importation into any EEC country, other than from another EEC country, is now banned, large numbers of the 1 ounce coin remain in circulation and may be freely traded. Coins can be obtained at almost no premium to the gold price but a seller should expect to experience a discount of around 1%.

A number of existing coins, though nearly all recent, have sought to fill the void left by the krugerrand. All are made in a series 1 ounce, 0.5 ounce, 0.25 ounce and 0.10 ounce, but not all these coins are widely circulated.

The maple leaf
This is the oldest of the newcomers, and is produced by the Royal Canadian Mint. It differs from the krugerrand in that it is made from pure gold, not an alloy. It does, of course, contain the same amount of actual gold as the krugerrand. The premium charged to a buyer of a 1 ounce coin would be about 4%.

The Australian nugget
Produced and marketed by Goldcorp Australia, Perth, Western Australia, whose ultimate parent is the Government of Western Australia, the nugget series has been particularly successful in the Pacific area.

Unlike other bullion coins, the nuggets have a frosted finish, with a different nugget depicted on each of the four coins in the series. It is also claimed to be the purest gold bullion coin available.

The premium charged to the buyer of a 1 ounce coin would be about 4%.

The American eagle

Produced and marketed by the Department of the Treasury, United States Mint, it has, like the nugget, yet to establish itself strongly in the UK. The coins, like the krugerrand, are made from 22 carat gold, but have the same gold content as all the other bullion 'series' coins. Again, expect to pay about 4% premium to buy a 1 ounce coin.

The Britannia

Coming to the market in late 1987, the Britannia is the newest of the gold coins. The Royal Mint's new coins will also be produced in a 1 ounce, 0.5 ounce, 0.25 ounce and 0.10 ounce series.

The UK sovereign

Before the advent of the krugerrand, the sovereign had wide circulation in many parts of the world.

Large quantities of old sovereigns (Queen Victoria, King Edward VII and King George V) were produced during most years of those reigns and sizable quantities of new sovereigns bearing the head of Queen Elizabeth II have also been produced. Sovereigns are made from 22 carat alloy and contain 0.2354 of an ounce of fine gold. Coins may be bought and sold at prices close to the gold content value.

It is worth noting that sovereigns and the britannia, when available, may be bought and sold so that any profit is free of CGT.

Most medium-sized branches of the four UK clearing banks will sell all or some of these coins. Alternatively, coins can be bought in large quantities through any of the five London bullion houses, who between them fix the price of gold twice a day. (Names and addresses are listed at the end of this book.) Spink, the coins and medal specialist, also sells bullion coins.

Individuals can trade gold in the futures market, although it is more complicated than buying coins or investing in shares and is really only suited to the sophisticated investor. The contract unit is 100 ounces on the New York Commodities Exchange.

Gold shares have an advantage over coins in that they offer a dividend yield. The most established market for gold shares in South Africa, where Anglo American and Consolidated Goldfields (fast diversifying into North American gold) dominate. Australia, Canada and the USA also have gold mining companies with trading shares. Here it is important to distinguish between the producing mine with proven reserves of ore and the speculative shares from a company, say, in Canada or Australia, which may have found some gold but is uncertain of the quantity or the grade.

For the small to medium-sized investor, the best way to invest in gold is through unit trusts which specialise in the metal and the mining companies. These have been performing very well of late but there can be no guarantee that this performance will continue. However, they do offer the advantage of leaving the decisions to the professionals.

41 What about investing in diamonds?

Investing in diamonds is fraught with danger for the unwary. In the late 1970s and early 1980s diamonds attracted a number of unscrupulous and short-lived investment companies, which quickly disappeared as the market went into recession. For that reason De Beers Consolidated Mines, which dominates the diamond market, believes the personal investor should restrict their investment to buying diamond jewellery rather than simple diamonds. Potential investors ignore the wisdom of this advice at their peril.

In terms of diamond output the world's largest producers (in order if size) are Australia, Zaire, Botswana, the USSR and only then perhaps surprisingly South Africa. Australia, Zaire and the USSR account for 83% of mined caratage. About half the stones produced are cuttable with the remainder being used as industrial diamonds.

I WHAT Investment

ONLY WINNERS NEED APPLY

Some people believe that taking part is more fun than actually winning. But now you can have the pleasure of both, with the magazine that puts you on the inside track every time. It's WHAT INVESTMENT, the friendly, informative monthly publication that takes the struggle out of making money. Just look at what you'll receive when you subscribe:—

* Decisive pointers on how to invest your money for the best returns.
* Hot tips from Joe Bloggs, the man in the street with the golden touch.
* Direct access to our exclusive telephone Investment Hotlines with up-to-the-minute news on what shares to buy ... and sell.
* The inside story on a different leading British company every month.
* Advice and recommendations on unit trusts.

Now, you can be a winner and have fun in the process, with WHAT INVESTMENT, the magazine that gives you a complete guide to what's going on in the world of money. ACT NOW ... SUBSCRIBE TODAY!

Name_____

Address_____

_____

_____

Signature_____ Date_____

I enclose a cheque for £22.60 made payable to Financial Magazines Ltd

Please debit my ☐ Access ☐ Visacard ☐ American Express

Card No. ☐☐☐☐☐☐☐☐☐☐☐☐☐☐☐☐☐☐

Please complete and return to: WHAT INVESTMENT, Subscription Department, 40-42 Campus Road, Listerhills Science Park, West Yorkshire, BD7 1HR.

WI 41

6 PROPERTY

● 42 Should I invest in property?

Property – whether housing or land – is normally the biggest investment an individual will make in his or her life. It is also an increasingly popular investment, with record numbers of individuals or families seeking home ownership. As the sums involved are beyond the financial resources of most people, they have to borrow money to buy the house of their choice. Building societies account for 70% of all the loans.

By and large, anyone who has invested in property over the last 20 years will have found it a good hedge against inflation, as house prices have for most of the period outstripped the growth in the cost of living. Moreover, there are significant tax advantages, in terms of income tax relief, in borrowing money to buy a home (the income tax relief covers the interest elements in the repayments on the first £30,000 of a loan at the borrower's marginal tax rate). And there is the added advantage that when you want to sell the house, not only is it a readily realisable asset but also the sale will not be subject to CGT for any profit you make.

In order that the mortgage interest paid to the lender may qualify for tax relief, the loan must be used either for purchasing a property or for improving it or for paying off another loan which itself was for purchase or improvement of the property or for the purchase of a share in a partnership, or a loan made to a 'closed' company. Two principal restrictions apply:

1 The property must at the time interest is paid be the only or main residence of the borrower, his divorced or separated spouse or a dependent relative, or be so used within 12 months of the loan being made. If the property ceases to be used as the only main residence, relief may continue for a limited period (normally 12 months) in respect of a loan on that property.

2 No relief for interest is due in respect of that part of a loan which exceeds £30,000. All previous similar loans which are still outstanding must be brought into account for the purposes of this limit, but an exception is made where a borrower moves house and temporarily owns two properties and on each of these there are loans outstanding.

Tax relief may also be obtained if the property is being purchased with a view to future occupation as a main residence by a borrower currently living in job-related accommodation. Interest may also qualify for tax relief where funds are raised against the security of the only or main residence of a borrower aged 65 or over and where 90% or more of the proceeds of the loan are used to buy a life annuity which will end with the borrower's death or, where there are two annuities, the death of the survivor.

43 What are the lending policies of the building societies?

Building societies provide loans to home buyers who in turn give a mortgage to their society. The mortgage is a legal charge on the property. The mortgage deed is the legal contract between the society and borrower. It comprises: the names of the parties to the contract, i.e. the borrower and the building society; a statement of the amount of loan being made and an acknowledgement by the borrower of receipt of the loan; a promise by the borrower to repay the loan with interest on the stipulated terms; the legal charge of the property to the society until the loan is repaid; and promises by the borrower concerning insurance and repairs.

When seeking a building society loan, a prospective purchaser can use the general rule of thumb that a society will be prepared to lend three times an application's gross earnings. If a joint loan to two people is wanted, the multiple may be three times the gross annual income of the higher earner plus once the other income. The building society will always want evidence of the applicant's salary from his or her employer unless an application is made for a non-status mortgage.

While societies will lend on all types of property, provided they are structurally sound, there could be problems with the following types.

Properties with a short life: Leasehold properties with 30 or less years to run before the lease expires are said to have a 'short' life. Most societies require the expected life of the property to be at least 40 years.

Leasehold properties: Societies will require that the lease should run for 20 to 30 years after the period of the loan.

Converted flats: Most societies will lend on converted flats as long as the conversion is structurally sound and the lease makes provision for maintenance and repair of common parts of the building. Also the property must have been completed under planning permission.

Freehold flats: These are not normally acceptable because of legal difficulties over repairs.

44 What different types of mortgage are there?

A proportion of home buyers elect to repay their mortgage loans by 'annuity loans'. These provide for regular monthly repayments so that over the life of the mortgage (normally 20 or 25 years) the debt, together with interest, is entirely repaid.

The alternative repayment method (now the favourite one with home buyers) is to link a loan to an endowment assurance plan. During the life of the loan the borrower pays interest only to his building society. Simultaneously, he pays a monthly premium to an insurance company. When the mortgage expires, the proceeds of the endowment policy are used to repay the building society loan; there could be some money left as a bonus for the home buyer. An endowment is a fixed term savings plan. The three types of endowment mortgage are:

Non-profit endowment mortgage: Where the proceeds of the endowment policy are sufficient to repay the mortgage loan and the borrower is left with no lump sum.

With-profits endowment mortgage: Here the sum assured is equal to the mortgage loan but bonuses mean that the borrower receives a substantial lump sum after the loan has been repaid. The proceeds may be up to three times the amount of the loan, which has the disadvantage that it is expensive for the borrower who is participating in a savings scheme.

Low-cost endowment mortgage: This policy assumes that the eventual proceeds of the policy (with bonuses) will be higher than the sum assured and so the initial sum to be assured is lower than the size of the loan. This has the advantage of reducing the premiums to be paid but you run the risk that the proceeds may not have appreciated enough to cover the loan and you will have to make up the difference.

The advantage of an endowment mortgage is that the loan will be paid off in full in the event of the borrower's death. But they have the disadvantage that when mortgage rates increase, the borrower cannot usually extend the term of his loan as most lenders are prepared to extend the mortgage terms. Higher repayments will have to be met in full.

Whether you have an annuity mortgage or an endowment mortgage, the system by which you obtain tax relief on the interest you pay is the same. Your building society calculates the amount of basic rate tax relief you are entitled to and deducts this from your monthly mortgage repayment. So the amount you pay your building society monthly will be net of tax relief. The Inland Revenue reimburses your building society with the difference between the net figure you have paid and the figure the building society would have asked you to pay had there been no tax relief on the interest element of your repayments. This is called Mortgage Interest Relief at Source (MIRAS).

45 What costs are involved in buying a house?

In an active market, you will probably have to offer the asking price for your chosen house, but where there are plenty of houses on the market you may be able to offer less. It would be helpful to know before you start house-hunting exactly what your maximum borrowing capacity is.

Offers should be made 'subject to survey and contract', which means neither side is legally bound to go through with the sale at this stage. It is at this point that the building society should be formally approached for a loan. You will have to give details about the proposed house, and about your financial background to confirm that you have the ability to repay the loan. The building society will want to check the value of the property and a valuer will be called in to do that. The fee is normally calculated according to the purchase price. You are strongly advised to have a structural survey carried out; this will usually cost approximately £200 plus VAT. It may be possible to combine the building society valuation and a full structural survey with a resultant saving in costs.

The building society makes an offer of advance based on the valuation of the property or the purchase price, whichever is the lower. Lenders can offer 100% mortgage but it is more common to put down a percentage of the purchase price – around 80% – but for this they will probably want some security. The rest you will have to make up from savings. If the advance exceeds 80% of the valuation, the building society will want more security. This is usually in the form of an indemnity by an insurance company for which a single premium is paid. The building society makes the arrangements and the premium is added to the loan. The loan will be unconditional, unless defects are found in the house, in which case:

1 The building society will offer the full amount of the loan on purchase but on condition that remedial work is done within a certain time limit.

2 The building society will only offer part of the loan, with the balance being paid when the necessary work is done.

3 The building society will offer a total retention if the work required is sufficiently major.

You will now need a solicitor to check the mortgage deeds and so on. This conveyancing of the property is an expensive business, though there is no longer a statutory scale of fees. As a rough guide, solicitors now charge a basic fee of about 0.5% to 0.75% of the purchase price, e.g. £150 if the price is £30,000 and so on. Solicitors have to abide by Law Society rules; they have to carry insurance and in turn are subject to close scrutiny from the Society.

If the land on which the house is registered (and 75% of houses are covered by registration), the solicitor's costs should be lower. A small charge is made for registering with the Land Registry – £50 to £175 on properties up to £100,000.

You can, of course, convey your property yourself or go to a licenced conveyor. However, if doing the conveyance yourself on an old property, do conduct thorough searches. If dealing through a licenced conveyancer, check to see that he carries insurance should anything go wrong. There have been instances in the past where these firms have gone out of business holding clients' money, with consequential loss to their clients.

Stamp duty is a Government tax on the purchase of houses. It has to be paid where the house price exceeds £30,000. The rate charged is 1%, a reduction from the 2% level prevailing before the March 1874 budget.

Of course, if you are selling a house you may have to pay an estate agent's commission which can be as much as 0.5%. For flats there are other disbursements such as for freehold (approximately £20) and for leasehold (approximately £40).

Other annoying factors when moving include delays, which can also occur if locked into a 'chain'. Local authority searches can take time and in some areas a wait of three months is not uncommon.

46 Is investing in a second home a good idea?

With property prices rising again, it might seem a good idea to get in to the second house market if you can afford it. Remember, though, that raising a second mortage could be difficult and when you sell it any profit will be subject to CGT. The advantage of a second home is that you can boost your income by letting it out. Although there could be liability to CGT, this tax, of course, is index-linked.

If let correctly, either by doing it yourself or by using estate agents (do obtain references on the latter and take these up), you could find that a net deficiency of costs 'set against your Schedule E income'. But it is not so much finding trustworthy tenants as making sure that you use the correct lease. It is vital in this instance to use a solicitor to check any lease recommended by agents (there are proposals to make considerable changes to the present practices). Agents' management fees can be as much as 15% of the rental income!

47 Is time sharing in the UK worth thinking about?

Time sharing developments in Britain are thought to be worth around £50 million, with some well-respected companies such as the Midland Bank, Wimpey, SGB, Barratts and Kenning involved. It all started in France in the mid-1960s and today there are around 1,100 developments worldwide. In England and Wales timesharing is restricted by law against perpetuity, which means that no time-share unit can be sold for longer than 80 years, nor can more than four people own a freehold property. However, across the border in Scotland, and in France, Spain and many American states, you can buy the freehold in perpetuity.

An important point to remember, as well as location (no-one wants to buy a timeshare in the Gorbals), is the actual time of year the property will be yours. After all, if someone was keen to sell you a month's holiday in the Yukon in January, would you take it? You should also bear in mind that resale could be difficult or certainly not fast.

Normally, periods of purchase are for an agreed number of weeks with a maximum of 12 being available. And remember that while it may appear to be a low-cost holiday option, there are management costs, which will rise with inflation or faster.

To determine who is a reputable timeshare agent, contact the British Property Timeshare Association, or the Time Ownership Trade Association, a rival of the BPTA.

The international exchange arrangements are vital and no one should consider signing any form of contract without the opportunity of taking legal advice.

48 Is it worth investing in a farm?

It is usually a balance of two or more of these reasons that justifies people's decision to buy a farm:

1 Income
2 Capital Growth
3 Security
4 Enjoyment

Dealing with them individually the following points are of interest:

1 Income: For a farm to be independently viable and efficient it now has to be about 500 acres or more (this varies with different types of farming, in other words a dairy farm can be viable on as little as 150 acres while hill sheep farms need to be substantially more. Current prices for commercial farmland are as shown on the table below.

Land is graded from 1 (the best) to 5 (the worst). In addition to the purchase of the farm, the farmer will need between £300,000 and £500,000 per annum approximately for working capital. He can expect to receive a return of between 2% to 5% on his investment capital and 10% to 15% on his working capital.

The main problem facing farmers at the moment is that of surplus and the still unresolved threat of commodity prices being cut and therefore profitability being reduced.

2 Capital growth: The prospects of capital growth depend entirely on timing. In the 1970s land values rose substantially (see table below) mainly due to the effects of inflation. Since the end of 1983 values have fallen back by anything between 30% and 50% on pure commercial farms. To get capital growth, it is important to buy at the bottom of such a cycle. After such a fall certain arguments are being put forward to the effect that we are nearing the bottom. The cheaper the farm becomes the better the return on capital.

3 Security: Agricultural land has always been regarded as a secure investment because if an investment goes wrong there is still something tangible that is owned. In the UK land is a limited commodity with a wide number of demands on it and its different uses. Security is of importance when there is uncertainty in the financial or political world. In times of stability the value of this is not so highly regarded.

4 Enjoyment: In addition to the business of farming there is the enjoyment of owning land and all the sporting and other amenities associated with the countryside. This market is particularly strong at the present time with large sums of money being generated in the City of London, industry and from abroad, all wanting to invest in country properties with a nice house and the right environment. There is also a demand for small areas of land for ponies, hobby farmers and the proprietorial pleasure that owning a farm gives people which is not much different to that of owning a garden.

Property

Values in this market have gone up by 15% to 20% each year over the last two or three years because opportunities to buy such land and property is always scarce. In both these cases the price paid bears little relationship to the commercial return especially where a large house can increase the value substantially. It is then inappropriate to think in terms of price per acre.

Taxation

In addition to the above, there are attractions to own land for CGT and IHT reasons subject to certain qualifications. The payments of these taxes can be deferred, halved or varied considerably. To get the full benefit of these it is essential that professional advice is taken because the rules and procedures tend to be complicated. Farming can also be tax effective because certain living costs such as cars, house sales, interest charges, telephones and so on can be deducted from the income before tax is paid if it is a justifiable business cost.

Commercial Farmland (price per acre)

		Summer 1986	Summer 1984
Grade 1	Silt farm	2500-3500	3500-4500
Grade 2	Commercial farm	1400-1700	2400-2600
Grade 3	Commercial farm	900-1300	1800-2200

In Scotland recent sales would indicate the following range of values:

Class 2	Commercial farm	1200-1400	2200-2400
Class 3	Commercial farm	700-1000	1000-1400

Source: Savills.

Summary of Land Values 1976-86

Year ending 31 Dec	Income		Capital Values		Total Return		Retail Prices		
	Gross income index	Income growth % p.a.	Capital value index	Capital growth % p.a.	Total return index	Total return % p.a.	Retail price Index	Prices annual change	No. of farms
1976	100.0	22.5	100.0	27.2	100.0	31.2	100.0	16.5	180
1977	117.6	17.6	141.9	41.9	145.6	45.6	115.9	15.9	225
1978	136.9	16.4	192.7	35.8	202.2	38.9	125.5	8.3	269
1979	162.1	18.4	240.7	24.9	258.3	27.7	142.3	13.4	316
1980	186.4	15.0	228.9	-4.9	252.1	-2.4	168.0	18.0	362
1981	199.4	7.0	242.4	5.9	274.2	8.8	187.9	11.9	405
1982	220.4	10.5	237.1	-2.2	276.2	0.7	198.1	5.4	434
1983	237.1	7.6	240.1	1.3	288.6	4.5	208.6	5.3	439
1984	250.4	5.6	237.3	-1.2	294.6	2.1	218.2	4.6	435
1985	264.7	5.7	195.0	-17.8	252.2	-14.4	230.6	5.7	424
1986	273.4	3.3	156.6	-19.6	213.4	-15.4	239.1	3.7	396
1986-1986 annualised % growth		10.6		4.6		7.9		9.1	

Source: Savills.

49   Is it worth investing in Forestry?

Timber is the second largest import into the UK, currently standing in the region of £5 billion per annum. We import over 90% of what we consume. Recently a number of new highly efficient mills have been opened around the UK. These require a constant supply of timber to keep them running and therefore the buying of timber from both abroad and home has become more competitive resulting in timber prices going up. We are also vulnerable in that the countries we import from, in many cases, Commonwealth countries, have increased their own consumption of timber. These countries have also started to process timber before they export, increasing the price to us. Some countries have a poor forestry record and do not replant where they have previously felled, therefore reducing the overall reserves of timber available. The main countries affecting world timber supplies in the future will be Russia, North America and, to a lesser extent, Scandinavia.

The points regarding security and, to some extent, enjoyment, mentioned previously on agricultural land, also apply to forestry and although in many cases the income may not start to come in for

25 years or more, the capital growth and eventual income could look attractive. Forestry is definitely a long-term investment.

The UK is going through a stage of adolescence in woods in that many people can remember the land before it was planted and feel that the current thickets (15 to 25 years old) are impenetrable. There is therefore some resistance to this change in the appearance and access that results; however, as these woods mature (following a major planting programme after World War II), they will become more accessible and attractive. Some of the older forests in the UK are major public attactions, i.e. The Forest of Dean, Thetford Forest, and so on. It is important that the balance between the need for commercial woods and enjoyment of the countryside by everyone is sensitively kept by those involved.

Publicity has been given to the tax advantage available to planting woods. In simple terms, if correctly managed, the expense of planting commercial woods can be set against tax on other income and the revenue produced from felling trees can be received tax-free. Timber is free of CGT and there are substantial benefits for other CGT and IHT management. This again is a subject that requires careful professional advice as it is a complicated matter.

Forestry does appear to be a logical alternative use of land (amongst many others) at a time when there are problems to be solved in the EEC agricultural policy.

7 SMALL BUSINESS

50 What are the advantages of investing in small businesses?

'Small is beautiful' is a sentiment the Conservative Government has embraced with great enthusiasm in Britain when it comes to supporting business. And many would say, not before time, too, since the small business sector in Britain is considerably smaller than in many of our more prosperous and economically more efficient competitors. Its share of manufacturing employment has risen from 27% in 1973 to 30% in the 1980s. However, this is still a long way behind the German figure of 32%, the Japanese of 68% and the Americans of 39%.

To encourage more small businesses (usually defined as companies under 200 staff) in Britain, the Government has developed a range of direct and indirect aid. Today there are many such schemes. The Government has already spent £2 million on advertising to promote some of its schemes; these include the Business Expansion Scheme (BES) and the small firms' Loan Guarantee Scheme (which are discussed in detail below).

Useful as these are to the small businessman, or the potential entrepreneur, you should be wary of any red tape involved in applying for them and the sheer bewildering number of schemes. Another possible deterrent to starting or financing a small business was the recession itself. After all, who wanted to start or back a business when markets were apparently flat and demand depressed? The answer was, encouragingly, many, many people. From 1980 to 1984, in spite of thousands of business failures (about 140,000 more UK firms started to trade than went out of business.)

There are failures, too. A small proportion of those backed under the Loan Guarantee Scheme go to the wall. While institutions back what they think is a good idea (always hoping for the 100 to 1 return that some of the backers of the original high

technology companies in Silicon Valley, California made), the reality can be the £1 million written off in a Norwich Union portfolio of 26 companies worth £4 million.

Most of the new small businesses are started in the South of England, according to a survey published in June 1983 by the monthly newsletter, *Venture Capital Report*. The survey of 429 projects found that 56% were established in London, the South-East or the South-West. It found that the average finance required by a starting business was £139,000; there was also a heavy bias towards manufacturing, with 44% followed by the service sector with 20%.

Putting money into a small business, whether it is your own or someone else's, is definitely to be considered an attractive investment, which will receive government encouragement and perhaps financial aid and tax relief. But do not invest in small firms just for the tax relief – the business has to be a good one in its own right.

51 If I want to start my own business, where can I get help?

Finance for setting up a business comes from the following sources:

1 The personal resources of the businessman/woman.
2 Equity capital provided from outside sources or under the Business Expansion Scheme (BES) – details are best obtained from Department of Employment Small Firms Centre.
3 Medium and long-term finance, including leasing and hire purchase.
4 Banks.
5 Trade credit.
6 Government finance.

It is usually best to combine sources if at all possible.

Full details of different Government schemes can be obtained from the Department of Trade and Industry or any of its regional offices. However, some of the schemes merit special mention here.

Business Expansion Scheme: Individuals can claim tax advantages up to a maximum of £40,000 invested in small companies in any one fiscal year, though the relief flows through only when the money is out of the fund and is invested in the recipient company. A person paying the top rate of tax at 75% can thus invest, say £40,000, and it will cost him £10,000 net. A standard rate taxpayer paying £6,000 a year tax, for example, could wipe out his tax bill by investing something like £18,000. The BES does not apply to property and financial companies, or to companies listed on either the Stock Exchange or the USM. The investment must be held for five years.

Enterprise Zones: Over 28 of these zones have been set up round the country in depressed areas. Within the zones, new and existing firms will be exempt from rates and certain other taxes, and they will enjoy 100 per cent tax allowances for capital spending on industrial and commercial buildings. Planning procedures are to be simplified and remaining rules speeded up.

Loan Guarantee Scheme: This is designed to make commercial finance more readily available to small businesses which have been unsuccessful in getting finance on normal commercial terms. The Government will provide the lending bank with a guarantee for 70% of the loan and the lending bank bears the risk of loss on the remaining 30%. Applications can be made through a number of banks including all the main clearing banks as well as Investors in Industry (the newly re-named financial institution backed by the major clearing banks and the Bank of England). Applications can be made by sole traders, partnerships, co-operatives or limited companies already trading or just starting in business. Agriculture, banking and finance and public houses are among certain excluded businesses. A full list is available from any of the sponsoring bodies. Guaranteed loans can be for amounts up to £75,000 repayable over periods of between two and seven years. Interest rates are determined by the lender. A 2½% interest rate premium is charged on the guaranteed portion of the loan to cover the cost of the guarantee. Further details are now available from the Small Firms Division, Department of Employment, Steel House, Tothill Street, London SW1H 9NF (01-213 3000 or freephone 'Enterprise').

52 What help do the banks provide?

Banks and financial institutions can provide a 'package of finance' – small loans and share capital – which will result in the institution having a minority interest in the share capital (29% to 49%). They usually deal in amounts larger than £25,000. Most of the clearing banks and their merchant banking arms now have divisions dealing with this. Investors in Industry (also called the '3 iiis') have a long record of providing this kind of finance.

53 Do I have to go just to the Government or to the bank if I want help?

No, British venture capitalists are coming forward all the time. The term 'venture capital' was coined in the USA and refers to the original backers of the high technology companies in Silicon Valley, California. Around £300 million worth of venture capital money is now available in Britain for investment each year. About two-thirds of the venture capitalists are in the British Venture Capital Association, representing 33 of the major companies in the field.

If it is advice or other help you need beside finance, there are a plethora of schemes available. For example, the Abbey National, with the Industrial Society and Capital Radio, offers a year's free office accommodation to young entrepreneurs in a 'Head Start for Business' campaign. The Industrial Society offers unlimited use of its information service to companies with under 50 staff for an annual fee of £50. Similarly, the London Enterprise Agency provides advice in the fields of property, finance, marketing and innovation. The National Federation of the Self-Employed and Small Businesses covers all its 50,000 members with an insurance policy guaranteeing £1,500 worth of professional advice, if their affairs are subject to in depth investigation by the Inland Revenue.

There is also the Government's Small Firms Services – an information system which was established in 1972 solely for owners or managers or prospective owners of small businesses. It has expanded dramatically since then; in 1982 they received nearly double the number of enquiries received in 1981 – and some 282,601 enquiries were received in 1985/86.

Small Firms Centres

BIRMINGHAM
6th Floor
Ladywood House
Stephenson Street
Birmingham B2 4DT
(021) 643 3344

LIVERPOOL
Graeme House
Derby Square
Liverpool L2 7UJ
(051) 236 5756

BRISTOL
5th Floor
The Pithay
Bristol BS1 2NB
(0272) 294546

CAMBRIDGE
Carlyle House
Carlyle Road
Cambridge CB4 3DN
(0223) 63312

CARDIFF
16 St David's House
Wood Street
Cardiff CF1 1ER
(0222) 396116

EDINBURGH
Rosebery House
Haymarket Terrace
Edinburgh EH12 5EZ
(031) 337 9229

GLASGOW
21 Bothwell Street
Glasgow G2 6NR
(041) 248 6014

LEEDS
1 Park Row
City Square
Leeds LS1 5NR
(0532) 445151

LONDON
Ebury Bridge House
2-18 Ebury Bridge Road
London SW1W 8QD
(01) 730 8451

MANCHESTER
3rd Floor
Royal Exchange Buildings
St Ann's Square
Manchester M2 7AH
(061) 832 5282

NEWCASTLE
Centro House
3 Cloth Market
Newcastle-upon-Tyne NE1 1EE
(091) 232 5353

NOTTINGHAM
Severns House
20 Middle Pavement
Nottingham NG1 7DW
(0602 581205

READING
Abbey Hall
Abbey Square
Reading RG1 3BE
(0734) 591733

54 If I want to start my own business, what are the pitfalls to avoid?

The first point you must remember is that although it is a daunting prospect to leave the shelter of a salaried position within a large organisation, the rewards of running your own business and being the boss can be immense and not simply in financial terms. Job satisfaction is normally much higher (helped by the fact that a successful entrepreneur can quite literally make an eventual fortune by floating his company on the stock market).

That said, there are a lot of risks. First, small businesses must be run on a sound financial footing. Many apparently excellent firms with splendid products go to the wall because they have over-extended themselves. This can be overcome to some extent by bringing in outside expertise, and if you go to venture capitalists for support they will adopt a 'hands-on' approach, i.e. they will put management as well as money into the company. Remember always to shop around in the venture capital field if you have a good idea, since the days have long gone when British entrepreneurs were starved of resources. While the venture capitalist will charge a higher rate of interest on a loan or demand a stake in the company (which is fair enough, as you are by the nature of things a high risk investment until you have a track record), you can get different terms by asking around in the venture capital market, such as lower loan terms of a smaller stake demanded in your company. And while you will have to work much harder than you ever did in the past, the incentive will be simply that you have probably had to commit everything you have to venture, including your house. This is quite normal. Why should an entrepreneur expect anyone to back his business if he is not prepared to do so himself? It is an excellent motivator.

In running your own business, you will need a clear idea of what you are trying to do when, how much it wil cost, the market share you hope to achieve; in other words, a complete business play. It is no good just having a few bright ideas and a Double First in Genetic Engineering from Cambridge, without having a clear idea of how your biotechnology company is going to operate. Help in working out a business plan will always be given by a venture capitalist or any other potential source of support including a Small Firms Service Counsellor.

● **55   Can I invest in small businesses through a managed fund?**

The traditional route is via one of the specialist unit trusts that look for good small companies to invest in, ones normally quoted on a stock exchange. There are a number of these. M & G have the Smaller Companies Fund and the American Smaller Companies Fund. Save & Prosper have the Smaller Companies Income Fund, and there are many more. Advice on which to join should be obtained from your broker. Since the summer of 1983 a number of funds aimed at exploiting tax relief under BES were launched, and have proved quite popular.

The BES has opened up a whole range of new opportunities for the private investor who wants to get into small businesses. Taking advantage of the tax relief proposals with investments in unquoted companies, City institutions are now offering a range of funds. BES investments can, of course, also be made direct.

Aside from these funds, if you want to invest direct into a small business, one way is via the USM. But, as we have said earlier, it is usually an expensive investment unless you can get the shares in the original placing.

If you are wondering whether to become a venture capitalist on your own, the simple answer is do not. It is expensive, very risky and requires a great deal of expertise. However, those venture capital companies in the USA who go for a 'hands-on' approach and wait for up to ten years to reap the rewards of their investment are normally hoping that they will recoup ten times their original stake, which is a very good rate of return indeed.

8 PUTTING MONEY ABROAD

56 What are the first things to consider?

Since the relaxation of exchange controls in 1979, investing abroad to make money has become a feasible option for the investor. But that said, remember the following points:

1 Many other countries may not have similar policies and it could be difficult to remit your money back to the UK. In general, you are advised to go to OECD countries because Third World countries can provide problems.

2 Political stability, which we take for granted in the UK and which underpins economic prosperity, is often rare. A volatile country makes for nervous investors. Your investments are liable to nationalisation or destruction at the whim of a regime operating outside the normal rules of commerce.

3 Information about the country, its economy and price sensitive information may not get to you quickly enough for you to react, or language problems might intervene.

But bearing that in mind and assuming you take professional advice, be it from a British broker with a good reputation for overseas expertise or a bank or overseas broker with an office in London, do not forget that many overseas markets have done very well in the past. Sunrise economies of the Far East (Singapore, Hong Kong, Korea but not currently Japan) stand out here though it should be noted that there are certain limitations in investing in Korea and Taiwan. Growth rates of 8% to 10% a year have been commonplace and though the figure may not match that now, it is certainly a lot higher than the British rate.

57 When travelling abroad, is it best to buy currency before I go?

The answer to this question depends on the country. You will get a better rate by buying the strong or 'hard' currencies in Britain before you go overseas. This is because the hard currencies (at present the US dollar, the deutschmark, the Swiss franc) are sought after in the UK, whereas sterling is less desirable in the hard currency countries. So British banks will give you a better rate. The reverse is true of the 'soft' or 'weaker' currencies (which currently include the Belgian franc, the Spanish peseta, the Portuguese escudo and the Italian lira). These are better bought when you arrive at your foreign destination, where the banks or financial institutions will be more glad to get their hands on sterling than British banks are to be given the weak currency.

When actually changing the money, the best place to do so, whether at home or abroad, is always at a bank. The hotel or *bureau de change* charge a higher fee and you will get an even worse exchange rate than at your bank.

When going abroad with travellers cheques it is always preferable to take the local currency. This should ensure that you pay the 1% commission for traveller's cheques only once and you will not have to pay again to change them.

58 Can I make money by speculating in foreign currencies?

Yes – but it is a nerve-racking and very fast moving market which is best left to the professionals. If you sell currency at a profit as a UK resident, you will pay CGT subject to the annual exemption prevailing at the time. This rule applies unless you can prove to the Inland Revenue that the profit arose on an account held in a foreign currency to service a commitment in that currency – to pay foreign rents or taxes, for example. The Inland Revenue is hardly going to accept that a fixed-term deposit account in a foreign currency was held for such a reason. If you sell currency at a profit whilst not resident, you will have to pay CGT. This is, of course, subject to the 36-month rule – the necessary period of non-residence before attaining non-resident status through emigration, although this will have effect retrospectively. Indeed, if you are working under a contract of full employment, this 36-month period may be shorter (see question 63).

You can open a foreign currency bank account with a British bank, or with a foreign bank, but it must be declared to the Inland Revenue. You can speculate on currency markets through the financial futures market (see question 36).

59 Should I buy property overseas?

Only if you do it through a reputable British agent with impeccable overseas connections. There are a lot of unscrupulous people in the field and the property laws vary widely between countries. Do not forget that currency movements can wipe out any capital gains.

Spain has been considered a cheap investment at certain times. Anything over £20,000 may be worth buying, but it must be on a prime site, near a leisure complex. Villas on the Costa del Sol with three to four bedrooms and swimming pool are naturally more expensive – fetching £150,000 or over.

The American property market can also offer good opportunities. But again, check with a reputable agent and consider local taxation consequences.

60   Is it easy to transfer money abroad?

Any bank can do it for you through an international money transfer or an express international money transfer (via a telex) in both sterling and foreign currency. Another way to do it is to buy a banker's draft and remit it to a third party or your own account, and the bank overseas holding your account will pay up when you show proof of your identity. The charges for this service are reasonable. The money order or draft normally costs £2.50 for every £1,000 sent abroad. The minimum charge is £4 and the maximum irrespective of the sum is £30.

61   Can I open a foreign currency bank account?

Yes, you can do it at any British bank – both as a current and as a deposit account. The charge for this may vary from bank to bank and may be more than that involved in an ordinary sterling account. You can also open accounts at foreign banks, which will involve charges and procedures according to that institution's domestic laws. Such accounts must be declared on your tax return. For those travelling regularly abroad or investing overseas, having a foreign currency account can be helpful – but currency movements can be highly volatile, so you need to be aware of the risks.

62   Can I invest in overseas stock markets?

Yes, although the London Stock Exchange, along with the American and Japanese markets, is one of the most important in the world, there are opportunities for the British investor to cash in on profitability of foreign companies on overseas exchanges. As a general rule, when investing on a foreign exchange it is important to take into account not just the share price but crucially the currency and interest rates. Any gain in a share price can be quickly wiped out by currency movements.

Investing overseas has its particular advantages. First, there are special situations of which you can take advantage and which you do not get in the UK too often. For instance, French champagne companies are always worth considering in a good year for champagne. Second, yields are sometimes better overseas than in the UK. Third, by going overseas it is possible to move into countries in different parts of the economic cycle at different times. So you should be able to keep your investments in recovery or booming stocks and get out when you think the market has peaked.

There are, of course, disadvantages. First, the market hours may be limited to a couple a day (this is especially true in Europe), though this can be somewhat overcome by after-hours dealing through brokers. Second, there are some extremely 'heavy' stocks with prices that are way beyond the reach of the average investor. One Swiss drug company recently had a full share with a value of £26,500, though there were one-tenth shares at only £2,500. Third, the cost of dealing in Europe might put some private investors off. There could be a double commission to pay not only to the British broker but to an overseas broker as well.

Delivery and settlement is now far smoother than it used to be, though the Spanish and Italian markets are still far from satisfactory and experts advise giving them a miss. It could take a week to get all the documentation to those countries and often the only way to do it is to hand deliver when on holiday. In addition, Italy has stringent rules whereby the investor has to put cash up-front before dealing in the market. Generally it pays to have a UK broker – even if you are dealing in overseas stocks.

Germany: This is the fourth largest market in the world after the UK, Japan and the USA. It is not any bigger than this simply because much of German industry is owned by banks or in private hands and also because the eight German stock exchanges have a much more limited role than London in financing the corporate sector. Only 0.5% of total company financing comes through issuing shares (the main source of money being the banks). Turnover on the German exchanges is low because holdings are concentrated and major shareholders are not in shares for a quick profit. Germany has not been very rewarding lately to investors. In 1980-81 the squeeze on corporate profits was the most severe since the Second World War, with a real decline of 25% in 1980 and again in

1981. But Germany now has potential because as a trading national it will normally benefit from any upturn in world activity.

Switzerland: There are few restrictions on foreign investors and free trade. This makes it attractive for foreign investors. But as in Germany, it is the long-term investor who is most commonly found.

France: The stock market has suffered far less under a socialist regime than was originally feared, though the market has reacted badly to some of the austere measures announced by the Mitterand Government. The French market actually received a boost with tax concessions for domestic investors (the Loi Monory). These added some 800,000 participants to the equity market. With the privatisation of nationalised companies, a rapid ownership has started to occur.

The Netherlands: Though large for the size of the economy, the market has had a diminishing number of listed companies (down by 200 in 10 years). This is because Dutch companies prefer to raise money via private loans from the financial institutions. International companies actually outnumber domestic ones in the listings of the Dutch market.

Scandinavia: The market here has been active lately. The Stockholm market was among the world's top performers in the early 1980s because of foreign capital pouring into that country, tax relief, devaluation of the currency and share savings schemes. Foreign investment in Sweden is restricted by regulations governing the purchase of Swedish shares by non-residents. Norway, by contrast, finally abolished restrictions on UK investors in the spring of 1982.

The USA: Here there are no exchange controls and the market is huge. The British investor should note the different types of market. At the top is the prestigious New York Stock Exchange (NYSE), dealing in about 1,700 stocks, such as IBM, General Motors, and so on. Then there is the American Stock Exchange dealing in stock which is not quite as active as on the NYSE. A computerised national market also exists; this is known as the 'over-the-counter market' (OTC), dealing in perfectly respectable shares. And many stocks can be traded on the floor of regional stock exchanges also, such as the Kansas City Exchange and the West Coast Exchange.

Charges in America for dealing have been negotiated since 1975 when fixed commissions were abolished. Provided the investor knows which share he wants, he can save himself the expense of supporting a costly research effort by dealing through an 'execution boutique'.

Japan now has the biggest equity market in the world. The previous holder of this accolade was the USA, which has a very large equity market. However, British investors should not forget US disclosure laws. Depending on the percentage of shares held, ownership will have to be declared. Federal laws require disclosure if 10% of the company's shares are held, though some states require disclosure for as little as 1%.

Japan: The Tokyo equity market is dominated by the 'Big Four' securities houses, Nomura, Daiwa, Nikko and Yamaichi. These companies combined account for around half the trading volume. Nomura is by far the largest, accounting for nearly one-fifth of trading volume on the Tokyo Stock Exchange itself. All the Big Four have London offices offering research in dealing facilities for private investors in the UK. Nomura in London, for example, offers regular seminars and portfolio planning, organises trips to Japan for its clients and a comprehensive list of publications and a telephone advisory service to help clients keep in contact with Japan.

Hong Kong: This is regarded as a very volatile market, despite the recent agreement between the Chinese and British Governments on the colony's future. But a good dealing profit can be made.

For investors wanting to get into Europe, certain brokers, such as James Capel and Kleinwort Grieveson, are particularly strong in the field. Alternatively, the unit trusts in Europe include GT European, London & Brussels, S & P European, Henderson European, M & G European, Schroder Europe, Hill Samuel European, Barrington, Murray-Jonstone European, and Stockholder European. Brokers with a strong Japanese interest include Phillips & Drew and Vickers da Costa. You will probably need to put up between £6,000 and £7,000 to invest directly in Japan. American brokers with a strong British presence include Merill Lynch and Salomon Brothers.

● 63 Is it advantageous tax-wise to work overseas?

In general, British citizens who work abroad under full-time contracts of employment can save a great deal of money. Usually the jobs they go to are advertised as having a tax-free income and it is in this way that savings are made. So far as the UK is concerned, however, there are pitfalls to watch out for. Any individual who leaves the UK for full time service abroad under a contract of employment will be regarded as non-resident for that period, excluding the day of departure from and the day of return to the UK if:

1 The absence encompasses at least one complete UK tax year (6 April to 5 April following).
2 All the duties are performed abroad or any duties performed here are incidental to duties performed abroad.
3 Interim visits to the UK do not amount to six months or more in any one tax year or three months or more on average.

The possession of a home or 'available residence' has in these circumstances no significance unless the individual has remained a director of the UK parent company. If this has occurred then any duties performed in the UK are unlikely to be regarded as incidental. In the latter case the availability of a UK 'available residence' will prejudice non-resident status but generally it will not have any effect whatsover.

Rents received from letting your home in the UK will be assessable for income tax, indeed tax should be deducted at source by the tenant or agent after due allowance for relevant expenses, interest and depreciation of furniture, fixtures and fittings.

Dividends from UK companies will continue to be subject to UK tax although some government securities may well be exempt. Foreign securities will not be subject to UK tax whilst you are non-resident. Local tax regulations should be observed and allowed for.

Tax will in all probability, not be demanded on deposit interest (extra statutory concession B13) and a non-resident is not liable to the Composite Rate Tax, which is usually accounted for at source. It may well be advisable to retain surplus funds on deposit offshore and to close these accounts prior to your return to the UK in order to avoid any possibility of the interest being assessed to UK taxation after your return.

64 If I do not wish to sell an asset before I return home, how can I ● reduce my CGT commitment?

The first rule to remember about CGT is that the higher the acquisition value, the lower any potential CGT assessment will be. For such assets as share and unit trusts, 'bed and breakfasting' is a legal and often viable tax avoidance ploy. By arrangements with your broker or banker, assets are sold at the end of one day's trading and re-acquired at the beginning of the next, hence one term. Provided such an exercise is carried out whilst you are non-resident, you will avoid CGT and a higher acquisition value is established for future CGT purposes. Under Extra Statutory Concession D2, sales of assets are exempt if made during a period of non-residence even if the sale is made during a period which represents part of the tax year for the balance of which the individual is resident in the UK.

It is important not to undertake artificial transactions without obtaining professional advice as to the possible consequences. Similarly where the assets in question have been received as a gift within the last six years, and CGT has been held over at the time of the gift then this tax liability can arise.

But is this an opportunity to avoid IHT? Briefly speaking, no. The liability to IHT depends not on residence but on domicile and this cannot be changed as easily as residence.

9 ART, ANTIQUES AND OTHERS

● **65   When is the best time to buy art and antiques?**

The art and antiques market had a bad time in the early 1980s, like most alternative investments. This has been reflected in falling profits and cuts in staff rolls at some of the more prestigious auction houses such as Sotheby's. But, by mid-1983, with a return of the Conservative Government, a stock market boom, economic recovery and a weak pound, the market picked up. A number of German buyers have been noticed at British sales, taking advantage of the cheap pound. At the time of writing, the market in London looked quite strong, and it is contributing well over £50 million to Britain's invisible trade balance. However, like other markets, sentiment can change rapidly, so a prospective buyer or seller has to keep an eye on prices and trends. But in the longer term, prices of quality items tend to rise, so short-term timing is less crucial.

● **66   How do I choose what to buy?**

Always buy the best you can afford; quality rather than quantity. And always buy what you like. Even those who profess to have no interest in collecting or appreciating art and its offshoots will often find that when they are guided towards a possibly good investment they will actually not be able to bear the idea of having it in the house, so a process of elimination occurs.

Areas which have suffered and where the market has collapsed are those which were used mainly for investment and were subject to the same volatility as the stock market. Collectors, on the other hand, keep on buying as long as they can afford it, so these goods have a longer-term price stability.

67 Is it best to make a collection?

A collection will always fetch a better price than a number of totally unrelated pieces. You can collect anything; make it an interesting and coherent collection that catches your interest and it will, perhaps, catch the interest of a buyer when you wish to sell.

68 Is attribution important?

It makes a lot of difference to the investor. The danger is, of course, that after a few years, a work of art may be downgraded and become classified only as 'thought to be by . . .' or 'school of . . .' To be mercenary, the only valuable thing about a work of art is who it is by. Some well-known forgers, however, are eminently collectable, but they are for interest value rather than anything else.

69 Where do I go for advice?

It is important to read up as much as possible yourself before venturing into the field. Once you have decided on ancient Brazilian teapots, subscribe to the *Ancient Brazilian Teapot Monthly;* a list of relevant publications will be available at your local library who will also order for you any books that you need. Otherwise, go to one of the auction houses and speak to their resident expert, who is dying for the opportunity to discuss one of his pet subjects and will love telling you all about the said teapots. Your local antique shop may be helpful, although it is a good idea to do your homework first. Is it a member of one of the three main associations – The British Antique Dealers' Association, the London and Provincial Antique Dealers' Association, or the Society of Fine Art Auctioneers? If it is, then this suggests that the owner has some sort of good reputation. If the dealer is friendly and interested, cultivate him. He will be able to look out for pieces for your collection, advise you about authenticity, and generally help you with advice.

Contact another collector, if you can.

● 70 Are auction houses better than dealers?

Auction houses have less of an axe to grind. They do not own the pieces, and are interested in maintaining their reputation, and earning their commission. They too can make mistakes, but it is in their interests to be scrupulously honest. There are guarantees on certain things. If you can prove within a specified period – something like five years, but it varies – that the cataloguing description of an object is wrong, then you will get your money back. Remember though, that there is a complex grading of attribution that affects the value. If it says 'thought to be by . . .', or 'school of . . .', then you do not have much of a leg to stand on. If it states categorically that it is a Canaletto, and you can prove beyond reasonable doubt, backed by expert opinion, scholarship, scientific tests, that it is not, then you are covered.

● 71 How does an auction house work for me if I want to buy or sell?

There are two ways the auction house will be notified of prospective vendors. First, the private vendor can bring a sales item to one of the auction house branches scattered around the country (Phillips has 18) or alternatively the auction house is approached by both professionals and private individuals (such as solicitors, executors or estate agents) and can give a whole range of advice on taxation, investments, probate, house sales, valuations, and the best way to sell an item and realise an asset. The auction house will then send a valuer to see the prospective vendor and he will give a verbal valuation for an item to be sold or a written valuation for insurance probate.

The auction house arranges for the carriage and insurance of goods to its premises, where they are directed to the relevant specialist department and meet up with the goods brought in by the private vendor. The items are examined and valued by specialists, photographed, and selected for a suitable sale. This may be just an ordinary sale or it can be a highly important sale. Recently, for example, a sale at Sotheby's of Impressionist and Modern Paintings beat all previous records when £23.2 million was raised.

Items are allocated a lot number and described in the sale catalogue. It is now the turn for pre-sale publicity to swing into action. Advertisements and press releases are sent out to all the relevant papers or magazines. Catalogues are sent to all relevant subscribers, dealers, museums or libraries. Viewing can be arranged before the sale and sealed bids will be accepted from those who cannot attend in person.

After the sale, the vendor should receive payment within two to three weeks outside London, and within a month from London sale rooms.

Commissions charged at the main auction houses

Bonhams
Buyers: 10%
Sellers: private 12%
                10% after £500
Trade 6%

Christie's
Buyers: 8%
Sellers: 10%
South Kensington: 15% to seller only

Phillips
Buyers: 10%
Sellers: 12.5 up to £500
       10% over £500
Trade by negotiation

Sotheby's
Buyers: 10%
Sellers: private 15% up to £500
             10% over
Trade: 10% up to £500
      6% over

72 Where do I keep the pieces once I have bought them?

That depends how big they are, for one thing. Bear in mind that if you live in a modern bungalow with modest-sized rooms, antique French furniture or large canvases are impractical, to say the least. If they are very good examples, then museums may be happy to take them on loan, which is useful as they will undertake the cost of keeping and insuring them.

It also depends on how replaceable they are, and what condition they should be best kept in. For example, some of the Impressionists painted on wood, so if you hang such a painting above a radiator then its life will be considerably shortened, your investment will go up in smoke, and you will have ruined a beautiful object. French furniture is seriously affected by central heating, too. If you have a large house, with room for a gallery, or rooms that are large enough to keep objects in them, without heating and with care, then fine. If not, think about collecting glass, or silver, or other more manageable items. If the items are delicate, keep them out of reach in a glass-fronted cabinet. If you do not trust the children or the dog, do not buy them, or keep them in a safe, perhaps even in the bank. If they are irreplaceable, because of their rarity or their sentimental value, it would be foolish not to keep them in the bank. Jewellery, for example, can either be copied in paste for wearing, or can be taken out and worn on special occasions.

73 What about insurance?

In every case, and particularly if the objects are very valuable and/or portable, insurance is vital. *Check you household insurance.* It is often woefully inadequate. Most insurance companies give no cover unless there is adequate security. Some insist on a wall safe. Others will not have anything to do with you unless you keep your valuables in a bank vault. Others specify a burglar alarm as well, linked to the police station. If you have already spent a substantial sum on buying it, it is ridiculous not to spend the extra few per cent on keeping it safe. Do not expose your property to risk: take a lesson from the experts. Protecting its valuables is one of the reasons why the art world is so secretive.

74 How do I find out how much a piece is worth?

If you have been keeping an eye on prices, and think that the time has come to realise your treasure, take it along to your friendly dealer/expert/auction house. All three will be on the ball. The auction house will charge nothing for a verbal valuation, but it will only be rough. If you want a written valuation, either for interest or tax or probate purposes, which they will stick to, it will probably cost 1.5% of the price up to £10,000, 1% from £10,000 to £100,000 and 0.5% after that. If the piece is too big, then bring in a photoraph with a note of its measurements. If it looks interesting, an expert will come and have a look at it if you pay his expenses.

If you want to sell something very rare, and you are among the three people in the country collecting Brazilian teapots, go to one of the auction houses. If they think they can sell them, they will accept the pieces on a reserve basis. This means that a figure is agreed, below which you will not go. If the pieces do not fetch this price, they will be withdrawn. Commission will still be charged, unless you put them back in on a different date for less money, or unless you are a very good customer, in which case the auction house just may not have the nerve to ask you for the money.

75 Are rare books a worthwhile investment?

Yes. After a worldwide recession in 1981-82, the market is holding up. As one Christie's expert put it recently; 'Following the trend of recent years, some outstanding prices were realised for exceptional items which offset the lower volume of sales of both printed books and manuscripts in the 1982-83 season. The market remained steady for anything less than superb, but showed astonishing buoyancy when its appetite was whetted.'

For the future, plate books (botanical and topographical) and modern first editions are considered worth investing in, and for under £500 investors should go for signed limited editions of early literature. Some of Christie's sales have demonstrated the strength of the natural history market. Brookshaw's *Pomona Britannica* (1812) made £26,000, and a subscriber's copy of Lear, *Illustrations of the Family of Psittacidae or Parrots* (1832) went for £22,000. Political material is also climbing in value. One unpublished autographed letter by Marx accompanied by a letter from his son-in-law recently went for £5,508.

Rare books should therefore continue to climb in value. With careful selection the investor can continue to make the 18% compound annual return that rare book collecting made in 1980. Anything rare and unusual will always find willing purchasers.

76 What are the best hedges against inflation?

Results were found during a recent survey conducted by Phillips:

	Items strongest in demand in 1986	For 1987 buyers – items considered 'underpriced'
FURNITURE	Fine English period & decorative, especially lacquer & Regency. Fine 18C French. Best Edwardian. Windsor chairs. Dining sets.	Middle of the road Continental. Oak. Dutch marquetry. Cane furniture.
PAINTINGS	Highest quality in all fields. 16C-18C English portraits. Victorian marine & sporting. Top quality Impressionists.	15C/16C Italian. English portraits. Outstanding Victorian.
MODERN BRITISH PICTURES	Newlyn School.	Post-war artists. English surealists.
WATER-COLOURS	Good early & Victorian. Neapolitan gouaches. Scottish colourists.	Minor colourists 1790-1840. 19C portraits.
PRINTS	Good impressions. Decorative prints in period frames.	Minor Old Master prints. Modern British.
OBJECTS OF ART, CLOCKS, etc.	Garden statuary. Ivory sculpture. Fine animal bronzes. Tea caddies. Good longcase clocks.	Best 19C sculpture. Early & Renaissance metalware. Pewter. Bracket clocks.
CARPETS & RUGS	Good antique rugs. Decorative, room-size carpets, pre-1900. Caucasian.	Antique tribal rug especially Persian and Belouchi.
SILVER AND PLATE	Good flatware services. Good Victorian/modern coffee & tea services. Georgian chambersticks.	Georgian/Victorian cream jugs & mustard pots. Small collectables. Fine Sheffield plate.
JEWELLERY	Fine rubies, sapphires, emeralds. Georgian brooches. Named pieces, eg Cartier, Boucheron. Art Deco.	17C & 1950s gold jewellery. Gold & enamel items.
CERAMICS AND GLASS	English porcelain pre-1760. Good services. Early English pottery. Scottish pottery. Good French paperweights. Good Toby jugs. Staffordshire sporting figures.	18C English porcelain figures. Royal Worcester figures. Glassware, especially 18C English drinking glasses.
ORIENTAL	Japanese late enamels & Satsuma. Chinese export porcelain, especially armorial. Blanc de Chine.	Ivory carvings. Chinese enamel. Canton.
ART NOUVEAU AND DECO	Good pieces by renowned designers. Very good cameo glass. Bronze & ivory figures. Quality & rare Doulton.	Posters & certain graphics. Bronzes by lesser artists. Doulton animals.

Specialists' recommendations in 1987

To £500: Pedestal desks.
T0 13,000: Library tables. Early oak coffers. George III bureau bookcases.
Above £3,000: Sets of period chairs.

To £3,000: Dutch 17C portraits.
Above £3,000: Italian 15/16C primitives. English portraits.
Above £100,000: Impressionists.

To £3,000: St Ives school.
Above: Sickert.

Under £500: Pencil. Early monochromes. Illustrators.
To £3,000: European 2nd division.
Above: Early English watercolours.

To £500: Minor Old Master. Modern British. Foreign topography.
To £3,000: Best quality decorative.
Above: Museum quality, major masters.

To £500: Austrian cold-painted bronzes. Carriage clocks.
To £3,000: Chess sets. Music boxes.
Above: Marble statuary. Bracket & longcase clocks.

To £1,000: Tribal artefacts.

To £500: Claret jugs. Old Sheffield candlesticks & trays.
To £3,000: Good Victorian domestic silver.
Above: Canteens. Storr, Lamerie, etc.

To £500: Victorian gold chains & bracelets. Coral.
To £3,000: 1950s gem-set 'Cocktail' & 'Odeonesque'. Late-Victorian diamond brooches.
Above: Fabergé; signed Cartier etc.

To £500: Outstanding bargain is 18C English drinking glasses.
To £3,000: Fine-painted 19C English & Continental cabinet pieces.
Above: Top Meissen, English delft.

To £500: Japanese ivories. Ming bronzes.
To £3,000: 17C Japanese procelain. K'ang Hsi porcelain. Small jade.
Above: Good enamel & metal.

To £500: Jewellery by known makers. Doulton animals.
To £3,000: Lesser artists' bronzes.
Above: Bronzes by respected British sculptors.

MARKET CHOICE FOR 1987

Irrespective of their specialisation, Phillips specialists were asked to name items in the saleroom market they consider the best 'buys' likely to appreciate in value. appreciate in value.

Furniture claims the top place with the accent on fine English period and decorative genre. Edwardian is highly recommended – some Edwardian and Victorian has actually gone down in price because of a dip in US dollar support.

Level at second place are English **watercolours** and **modern British pictures** (notably paintings of the Newlyn school), two extremely buoyant sectors of the art market.

Three categories receive special attention because they are considered underpriced. English **drinking glasses** – mainly of the 18thC – are quoted as a 'splendid bargain'. **Pewter,** too, which has been in low demand, is regarded as an excellent buy at present. So are certain types of **silver,** including Georgian cream jugs and small collectables.

After the two main and separate areas of gilt-edged and underpriced opportunities, the specialists recommend: Ceramics (lesser English 18C, and English and Chinese blue & white), jewellery (Fabergé, Edwardian and deco), art glass and pottery, textiles including fans, golf memorabilia, toy soldiers, miniatures, Dinky toys, 19C Oriental bronzes, photographs, historical and commemorative medals.

The market at Phillips IN NEW YORK

Items strongest in demand in 1986:
Top European 19C paintings and watercolours. American Impressionists. First-rate American furniture. 20C German and Austrian pictures. Fine manuscripts/autographs on subjects, ie music, American History. 19C albumen-print photographs.

1987 buying – items considered likely to appreciate in value:
Federal furniture 1805-25. Good examples of works by second-rate Impressionists. Middle and lower range European paintings. Early 20C American art. 16/17C maps. 20C manuscripts/autographs. 20C photographic 'discoveries'.

OTHER SPECIALISED SUBJECTS & COLLECTORS' ITEMS	**In high demand:** European armour, Japanese swords. Oceanic artefacts. Musical instruments – fine bows. Botany, cookery & travel books. Royal, military & travel manuscripts. Early photographs. Globes & barometers. Needlework pictures & samplers; 18C costume. Royal ephemera. Golf books. Dolls' house futniture. Tinplate novelty toys. Teddy bear. Rare sets of Britain's toy soldiers. Model railside accessories. **Recommended for 1987:** Good English swords. Pre-Columbian pottery vessels. Violins by good English medium makers. 17/18C maps. English & Scottish local-history documents. Photographs of India. 18C fans; whitework christening gowns. Miniatures. Valentines. Football memorabilia. Corgi toy cars.
STAMPS	**In demand:** Classic European. GB 19C, fine or unusual. **For 1987:** National Postal Museum archive material.
COINS & MEDALS	**In demand:** Ancient Greek, Roman coins. Post WWII gallantry groups of medals. **For 1987:** Historical & commemorative medals. WWI campaign groups.

Source: Phillips, Fine Art Auctioneers.

77 What are the best bets outside furniture and paintings?

A survey of antiques (not included in the mainstream furniture and painting categories) by130 specialists at Phillips around the UK, Europe and North America highlighted the possible winners in 1985/86. See table on pages 102-3.

78 What about oil paintings, watercolours and prints?

The eighteenth century is a very popular investment choice with the experts, with modern British portraits and etchings also in demand. In paintings, nineteenth-century artists are attractive in the £6,000 to £9,000 range and, in watercolours, nineteenth-century Dutch artists in the £500 to £3,000 range.

Paintings are normally the showpiece of the auction houses and they divide their departments into several specialist areas to cover the whole field. Phillips, for example, sub-divides its pictures department into Fine Old Masters, Eighteenth and Nineteenth Century Paintings, Watercolours and Drawings, Fine Continental Paintings, Modern Continental Paintings, Modern British Paintings and Prints. And though paintings require a good deal of research and cataloguing by experts, this does not prevent a throughput of about 20,000 pictures a year in the Phillips sale room. Sotheby's and Christie's are larger but work in the same way.

The best advice on buying pictures is to buy because you like them. You will probably make money when you sell. And if you do not you will at least have had the pleasure of seeing the picture and will not be too put out if it does not sell. As a general rule of thumb for paintings, as interest rates fall and eventually go below the rate of inflation, then the art market will boom. People will prefer to put their money into appreciating assets rather than gilts or other government securities.

79 Which precious stones are worth investing in?

Provided they are of a fine quality, Burma or Ceylon rubies, Burma or Kashmir sapphires, Columbian emeralds, diamonds but of good clarity and colour, especially in the 2 to 4 carat size bracket. Semi-precious stones such as amethyst, garnet and peridot can be a good investment provided that they are in attractive antique gold settings.

105

Fashion dictates which stones are popular at any time. So does purchasing ability: you buy the best you can afford. If diamonds are too expensive, people turn to others. Recently, delicately-crafted pieces, often with relatively little spent on raw materials, have been fetching increasingly higher prices. Renaissance jewellery has been fetching prices in the region of £1,500 for necklace of glass beads and precious stones, set in gilt.

An attribution can easily double the value of a jewel. Prices for the work of makers such as Giuliano, Castellani and Falize have been high for years. Now other makers are attracting interest: a three-layer agate cameo of a bull being savaged by a lion was sold and identified as the work of a little-known nineteenth-century gem engraver, William Burch. It fetched £1,800 against a pre-sale estimate of £300-£500.

Jewellery, then, is a highly active and diversified investment field. If you decide to go into this field, acquire a 10x lens and familiarise youself with its use so that you can study allegedly flawless stones at first hand.

● 80   Which period of antique jewellery is best to buy?

It does not much matter but, to wear, Victorian and onwards is best. Collections are likely to be worth more than individual pieces. They also have a wider market than a flawless diamond worth a king's ransom. And, like the less expensive paintings, there is more chance that the less expensive pieces of jewellery will increase in value more quickly than the grander ones.

Naturalistic jewellery – animals, birds, flowers, trees – in perfect condition is popular at present. Regency, multi-gem jewellery sells well, although if a piece is repaired or modified, it is less valuable. Pieces are often set with sapphires, rubies and rose diamonds. Certain styles sell, notably those set with pretty stones or half pearls. 'Pretty' is the key description: that is what attracts buyers. Renaissance jewellery, when perfect, sells very well, and it is rare. Most pieces have been modified unskilfully which spoils the value and the look – you can always tell a piece that has been repaired or tampered with; try and sell it a few years after buying it, and you will be lucky to recoup your initial outlay. Cameos hold their value, if they are Renaissance onces, but are predicably rare. Roman ones, though older, are two-a-penny. Do not be misled by age.

81   Are furs a good investment?

The most beautiful furs have a natural life of something like 20 years. After that, the natural oils begin to dry out, and the garment begins to fall apart and look moth-eaten. Keeping it carefully in cold storage throughout the summer may increase its lifespan for a few years, but as an investment it is not a good idea to put your money into furs. There is also a strong lobby against the killing of animals for decoration. This has certainly affected some sales, and will probably continue to do so.

82   Are coins a worthwhile investment?

Many of the same principles apply to coins as to other alternative investments. They are a useful diversification, a long-term investment, and can make you money in the end. They too are subject to fashion, and to fluctuation in the market.

83   Where can I buy and sell them?

No one knows more about coins than Spink. Glendinings, affiliated to Phillips, are the specialist London coin auctioneers. Christie's and Sotheby's hold auctions about every month. Join a numistatic society (lists of these can be obtained from the British Association of Numismatic Societies). Subscribe to the two main magazines, who will keep you in touch with other collectors as well as provide information about what is going on: there are *Coin Monthly,* and *Coin News Incorporating Coins and Medals*. Cultivate the proverbial friendly dealer, but do not take a rare coin to an unknown dealer.

84   How can the coin market be affected?

By obvious things such as the recession, and everyone panicking and choosing to get rid of a particular sort of coin. A hoard of William I pennies discovered in 1833 immediately made the coin, previously one of the rarest, one of the most common.

The most popular coins at the moment are bullion ones such as krugerrands or sovereigns, or numismatic coins such as British,

ancient British, early Saxon or Norman and some hammered coins
(those struck by hand before 1662). These are rare collectors' items,
although it is important to get good advice from someone who
knows what they are talking about. It is important to go for quality
rather than quantity – coins in mint condition are the ones that
increase in value. At present, it is a buyer's market. There is a
shortage of rare and unusual material. Two years ago the
Americans entered the British market and prices soared to an
unrealistic level. They are lower but more steady now after
descending rapidly, and there is little sign of change or instability.

There is a British Numismatic Trade Association, to which
collectors and dealers belong, and they have an agreed code of
practice. They hold an annual fair in September or October.

85   Do medals make good investments?

Yes, but like all unusual investments, it depends on which medals
you choose. The really rare and most famous medals such as the
Victoria Cross are, by their nature, the most valuable. Because it is

the highest award for gallantry (founded by Queen Victoria in 1856 and made from the metal of guns captured at the siege of Sebastopol), only 1,348 have been issued. This has meant that the suggested minimum for a Victoria Cross has climbed from £1,500 in 1972 to around £10,000 today (though recent prices have varied from £7,500 to £110,000). The George Cross awarded for conspicuous gallantry (not in face of the enemy) is slightly less valuable. In 1972, one would fetch £600. Today, it might be £5,500.

Collectors usually start, however, with a Waterloo medal or others from the Napoleonic Wars, such as the Military General Service Medal with one of 29 bars covering different campaigns. Prices for these kinds of medals vary from £260 to £1,250 for the Fort Detroit Bar (for the American War of 1812). The table on page 111 gives an idea of how a range of medals has fared in the last ten years. Remember that inflation has pushed the cost of living up four-fold over the same period.

86 What are the points to remember?

As with all unusual investments, there are a number of points the investor should bear in mind:

1 The importance of research cannot be underestimated. It can make a big difference to the value of a medal. Whether a recipient of the Crimea Medal charged with the Light Brigade or not, for example, can make a difference of between £100 and £900 to the price of tht medal.

2 NCOs' and officers' medals are most costly because there is usually more biographical detail accompanying them. A junior officer's medal can be expected to have a 40% premium while a major's or a rank above will have a 100% premium.

3 Collectors like the medals to be kept in good condition (as soldiers wore them).

4 If the original naming of medals has been altered, it can have an adverse effect on the value. Renaming took place when the recipient's medal was lost or stolen and he did not wish to wear a replacement bearing someone else's name.

5 Defective medals or those that have been repaired should be avoided.
6 Re-issued or later issued medals are not as valuable.

7 Copy medals should be avoided – these will have been recently produced because of the increasing interest in medals.

87 Do memorabilia have investment potential?

Possibly, as you are in fact buying a 'future'. Something you buy now and keep may, in some years, become more expensive and more in demand. The person who sells a collection of Dinky toys is laughing all the way to the bank. The person who bought them may not make such a profit.

Good craftsmanship matters, and could influence prices in some years. The price reflects the balance of supply and demand.

Many outsiders suggest that auctioneers owe their own growth (which has been very good) to inflation-induced investment interest in antiques and fine arts. But the auction houses have greatly expanded the number of categories they handle. They regularly hold sales of anything they think might interest investors. This continuing expansion has not always made them popular with the dealers. In some respects, auctioneers are the wholesalers and dealers are the retailers. Wholesale sale prices are much lower than retail prices, so many collectors and investors are buying direct from the auctioneers. In some fields dealers have been virtually eliminated from the market.

88 Are toys and trains a worthwhile investment?

Yes, provided they are in mint condition – which usually means coming in their original box – and if they are 20 or more years old. The Dinky toys, which were produced in 1933 until the closure of the factory in 1979, are regarded as the classic collectors' items. Some of the prices they fetch are staggering. A 1933 Firestone van, priced at 6d then, would now fetch £300. A Mobil gas oil tanker from the mid-1950s, £300. Rarer items include the 1955 Vulcan bomber, worth £500. Dinky only made 500 in 1955 and ironically they did not sell very well then!

Electric train sets are another category where prices have been particularly strong. At a recent sale at Phillips (regarded as the best auction house for toys and trains), a Bassett Lowke 4-4-2 tank locomotive in near mint condition went for £1,400 against the £200 to £250 expected for it. Interest is not merely confined to models.

At the same sale a large collection of tickets from old railway companies, expected to make £60 to £100, reached £3,200. There is a hard core of 50,000 collectors in the toy and train field so there is plenty of scope for buying and selling. Investments will appreciate in value again as long as they are kept in mint condition.

Guidance on which toys might be good investments can be obtained from auctioneers.

Comparison of medal prices since 1976 with estimations for 1987

	1981	1985	1986	March 1987
	£	£	£	£
Victoria Cross (suggested minimum price)	8,000	10,000	9,000	9,500
George Cross (suggested minimum price)	3,000	5,500	5,000	4,500
Military Cross George V	100	125	110	–
Military Medal George V	45	55	45	48
Distinguished Flying Cross George V	220	275	200	240
Seringapatam Medal (Silver)	200	250	240	300
Mr Davison's Nile Medal (Bronze)	60	80	80	90
Mr Boulton's Trafalgar Medal (Silver)	465	525	600	700
Military General Service Medal Bar EGYPT	220	225	250	240
Military General Service Medal bar FORT DETROIT	1,000	1,250	1,250	1,400
Naval General Service Medal	875	900	800	750
Naval General Service Medal bar SYRIA	200	230	170	170
Waterloo Medal (Foot Regiment)	240	260	240	250
Crimea Medal Bar SEBASTOPOL (impressed naming)	70	85	80	80
1914 Mons Star	20	25	20	20
Army Long Service and Good Conduct Medal (Victorian)	40	50	30	35
Naval Long Service and Good Conduct Medal (Victorian)	60	70	40	40
Coronation Medal 1911	15	20	20	20
Coronation Medal 1953	20	25	25	25

It is, of course, important to go to a reputable dealer because he will guarantee the medals he is selling. Price trends may be assessed from attending auctions and from dealers' lists and catalogues.

The specialists in the field are Spink. Books to read include Major Gordon's *British Battles and Medals* (Spink); Edward Joslin, *The Standard Catalogue of British Orders, Decorations and Medals* (Spink; a new edition is forthcoming).

● **89 Should I invest in firearms?**

Only if you really know the business. A lot of unscrupulous people are trying to cash in on collectors' interest in the market by passing off replicas of old guns by distressing them (i.e. making the gun look much older than it actually is). Advice from experts is to buy only from reputable dealers and auction houses where fakes can be recognised and sorted out. When buying, go for the best quality and as good a condition gun as possible within your price range.

Certainly, you should not lose against inflation. Generally speaking, prices of all guns – whether old or modern sporting guns – have kept well ahead of inflation. Prices have increased by about

15% a year (although they did not do so at the depth of the recession in 1980-81). Cased pairs of duelling pistols are the best buys, though a recent sale of uncased Twigg pistols (the finest of all English gunsmiths) went for £4,000, double the market estimate. But in dealing in such pistols, it is important to ensure that they have not been converted from percussion to flintlock to make them appear older.

Modern breech loading and smooth bore guns (from 1890 onwards) are often bought by sportsmen who are interested not just in an appreciating asset but in using them. In this case it is vital, of course, to keep the gun well oiled and cleaned every time it is used or rust will eat away the gun and its value. There are many estab-ished gun-makers, like Holland and Holland, or Purdey, who can provide advice on some guns, or the auctioneers will provide expert opinions.

90   Are old cars a worthwhile investment?

Collecting old cars for investment started in a big way towards the end of the 1960s, when there was a huge boom in prices between 1969 and 1979. But the market came unstuck in 1979 and many experts have serious doubts about the 1979-89 period – so beware. The market appears to have been badly hit in the middle range of collectors' cars – the £15,000 to £40,000 bracket. Soaring resto-ration costs (£12 an hour labour and 1,000 hours work to strip and rebuild) have hit the market, together with the cost of garaging and repairs. But experts in the field stress that it is no good buying beautiful cars just to wrap them up and leave them in a garage. They will deteriorate rapidly. Cars must be used regularly, which in turn means regular maintenance. This can cost £1,000 a year with another £500 for garaging and insurance.

At the top end of the market, recession has little meaning for cars such as a Mercedes 500K Special Roadster, sold by Christie's in Los Angeles in 1979 for US$440,000. Even this price is dwarfed by the Bugatti Royale at circa US$6,000,000. Only eight were produced and six survive today. A bid of $2.2 million was made for one recently, but it failed. At the top 10% of the market, the prices have appreciated by an average of 30% for 20 years. European cars are the most valuable. American cars were produced in far greater volume and in any case are usually snapped up by American buyers.

Amongst recent prices, a Bentley R Type Continental 1952 is worth £60,000; a Bugatti Type 43 Transport 1928 £60,000; a Maserati 250F GP 1956 £100,000, a Rolls Royce Silver Ghost Alpine Eagle 1914 £65,000, and for a Mercedes Benz S Type 1928 you would pay circa £120,000.

Notwithstanding the risks involved (and many people thinking E Type Jaguars would be good investments bought them for £6,000 to £8,000 five years ago only to find they will probably get less than half for it now, the one area that experts believe will be worthwhile is in sports and sports racing cars.

Experts to consult include Christie's, Phillips and Sotheby's. Many cars appear at the top auction houses, who may charge 10% commission. There are also a number of antique car dealers in the Kensington area of London. Be careful, because they may include a large mark-up in the car's selling price.

91 Should I invest in old aircraft?

Aircraft are just starting to become investment items, but there is a limited market of aircraft types. Recent World War II films have increased the demand for Spitfires and Hurricanes. They cost around £10,000 to £20,000 then, and prices have rocketed since. For example, a Spitfire has recently been sold for £260,000. Peaks were set in the sale of the Strathallen collection two years ago. A Hurricane went for £260,000 and a Spitfire fetched £140,000. Spitfires and Hurricanes – because they are very well known – are regarded as the best investments. In the USA, the P51 Mustang and other World War II high performance fighters are similarly collectors' items (bigger bomber aircraft are not regarded as investments).

But there are drawbacks. The aircraft – like cars – need to be flown regularly to prevent deterioration. Running costs can be £800 to £1,000 per hour. Much of this goes on fuel (60-plus gallons an hour at £2.20 a gallon) and insurance premiums. Storage costs and the strict maintenance required by the Civil Aviation Authority (CAA) push costs higher still. The very stringent CAA rules do, however, make this sort of flying very safe indeed.

At the end of the scale, fabric and wood biplanes of the pre and early-World War II era have good potential for the future. Tiger Moths stand out here; four years ago they cost £9,000 to £10,000.

Today that figure is £17,000 to £19,000 and will continue to improve. Older biplanes of World War I vintage are too difficult to fly, they are very unstable and much too dependent on the weather. However, good examples present excellent value.

To find out more about the aircraft market, contact the large auctioneers, Phillips.

92 Is wine worth buying for investment?

Yes, on the whole, subject to luck and market fluctuation. However, the most important attribute for collecting and investing in wine is to like it, because, if the very worst comes to the worst, you can still enjoy drinking it.

Historically the best wines for investment have been claret and vintage port. Claret has always produced a more spectacular rate of return; vintage port takes longer. Stick to first growths in clarets and perhaps some second and third growth. This may cost from about £350 a case. The market crashed in 1973-74, but since 1975 it has been steadily improving. There are no signs of this changing. For example, Château Latour 1975 claret which has always had a good reputation was available for £150 a case in 1976, and now fetches £500 a case at auction. This is doing very well indeed, giving something like 20% compound interest. You are more likely to achieve 15%. Vintage port has been doing well recently.

When you buy, it is always best to get in early, when the annual growths are first offered. It will be about two years before they will be ready for shipping. There should be no problems about delay if you go to a well-constituted company, though there have been and still unfortunately are cases of even well-known companies becoming insolvent, in which case it is unlikely that you will ever see your wine, although you have paid for it in advance.

93 Do I need to know about wine before I start and where can I find out about it?

Most certainly, the answer is yes. This increases your enjoyment, and is also sensible. The Sunday Telegraph's *Good Wine Guide* is a good place to start. Hugh Johnson is prolific, and has produced several books. Michael Broadbent is Sotheby's resident wine expert, and has written *The Great Vintage Wine Book*. Other useful books include Jancis Robinson's *The Great Wine Book,* and Clive Coates' *Claret.* Advice is freely available from the auction houses and from reputable dealers.

94   Can I invest for other people?

You can establish a trust under Deed of Covenant thus achieving significant tax savings as well as laying down good wine for the future. The covenant is between the donor and the child (one generation removed). The child's parent or guardian is the trustee, and wines will always be chosen and invoiced to the trustee. It is possible for the investor to deduct income tax at the basic rate and for the parent and trustee to reclaim the tax on behalf of the child and add this to the investment, turning, say, £700 into £1,000. The maximum amount on which tax may be reclaimed is the child's income allowance and any income which the child is already receiving must be deducted from this.

Some wine merchants run investment plans offering differently priced selections of various wines for drinking in the future. The ones with the finest wines should show a healthy capital appreciation in the future, after about five of six years in reserve. The wines are bought young and kept. There is no point in buying good wine unless it is stored well. You can store wine either in a cellar or, if you do not have one, with a wine merchant. Contact a wine merchant for details.

95   Is it possible to share out the cost?

Forming a buying syndicate has benefits in terms of the discounts some merchants will offer for purchases of three or five cases, or ten or more. Be certain to sort out in advance who gets what, and if the wine is kept in the same cellar, issue duplicate records. You should keep records, in any case, of what wine you buy and sell. In the last war records of ownership were lost, and there are stocks of wonderful wine improving in cellars all over the country with no one to say who owns them.

96   Should I collect stamps?

Stamps have weathered the problems of the recession quite well and are regaining the ground that they lost. The independent survey, *Stamp Price Movements 1960-1983* compiled by the P & E Consulting Group, shows that even in the period 1980-83 stamps overall had a growth rate of 10% per annum. The Consumers Association's book, *Saving and Investing* (1982), showed stamps to be one of the most lucrative of the alternative investment areas.

Stamp 'collectors' are those interested in philately, while 'investors' often do not progress to becoming collectors. Advice is vital and it is better to go to an independent adviser, such as an auction house's resident expert.

Currently, Commonwealth stamps are popular. Other countries have their vogues – for instance, Rhodesia when it became independent, and the Falklands, more recently. Many of the higher-priced 'classic' items suitable for investment have now fallen and stabilised at their 1979 price levels, so it is a very good time to buy. All the recent auctions show that collectors are now buying these again, and are often paying more than the auctioneers' estimates. Ten years ago, the 1840 Penny Black, in top condition, would have sold for £20. At the peak of the market in 1979-80, the stamp would have sold for £300 and at the market's low in summer 1982 its value had fallen to £150. Recently, one sold at auction for £250. Stamps are a medium to long-term investment – up to ten years. In any given ten-year period stamps have always kept well ahead of inflation and offered attractive rates of return.

Stamp collecting should be thought of as a diversification; it would be foolish to put all your money into stamps, but for an investment of anything from £100 upwards, you can expect a reasonable return over ten years or so. When the market stabilises again, investors may be able to return to a holding period of five years. For safe investing, Stanley Gibbons recommend only classic items up to 1900 and certain items up to 1930 in very fine condition. Investors can, of course, make good profits on selective middle issues and more modern stamps, but this is more speculative.

An investor with Gibbons can choose either to place an initial sum with the company and add further amounts at regular intervals, and so build up an investment collection, or to buy an investment portfolio with a once-only lump sum. There is no charge for the service. Gibbons will either store and insure the stamps for you, at a

117

small charge, on a rising scale, or you can keep them in a bank. It is important to take care with the storage conditions – keep stamps flat and cool, at a steady temperature.

97 'D'ya wanna buy a horse?'

You can make money by investing in bloodstock but there is no guarantee of a profit on your investment. But then how do you value the pleasure and the fun derived from owning a racehorse?

An investment in bloodstock can mean either buying a racehorse, which is usually done at the autumn yearling sales, or making an investment in a female horse for breeding purposes, or buying a share in a syndicated stallion. Of these three alternatives, ownership of a horse for racing purposes is probably the most interesting and exciting. About 4,500 thoroughbred foals are born each year in this country, and just over half that number will race as two-year olds. The season for flat racing is from the end of March to the second week in November.

98   How do I buy a thoroughbred?

Enlist the aid of a reputable agency, such as The British Bloodstock Agency which is based in Newmarket and London. The
agency will advise on all bloodstock matters from purchasing and
insurance to registration and management. They charge a
commission of 5% of the purchase price.

Yearlings are bought at four main sales: Doncaster in
September, Goffs in Ireland in October and, the most important,
Tattersalls in Newmarket at the Highflyer Sales the first week in
October and then at the October Sales a fortnight later. But it is
essential to enlist expert advice when considering the purchase of a
racehorse.

99   What about tax?

Only a very small percentage of horses in training will win enough
to cover the costs incurred. If you own a horse as a private
individual you can legitimately claim to be following a hobby.
Winnings are free of income tax and as a horse is a tangible,
moveable asset with a life expectancy of less than 50 years, it is
therefore not eligible for CGT.

Value Added Tax (VAT) will normally be charged on the
purchase of a yearling as well as on the training fees.

100   Can I save on a horse's running costs?

You can buy a horse through a limited company, but remember
that you will need to register it at the Jockey Club in the horse's
name (which can refer to the company). It costs between £8,000 and
£10,000 a year to keep a horse in training. If owned by a syndicate of
private individuals the shareholder contributes to the cost of
keeping the stallion.

An exceptional male horse or stallion after its three or four-year-
old career is retired to stud, and there should be a huge demand for
him as a sire. Astronomical sums have been paid for syndicate
shares in such an animal. During the covering season, a stallion
would be put in with 40 to 50 mares, which in total would require 110
to 120 coverings.

The stallion is divided into 40 shares, giving each shareholder the right to send a mare each year to the stallion, or to sell his nomination to another mare owner. If mating is successful, the foal will be born 11 months later. One year on, the horse is sold at a price reflecting its parentage. After another year the horse will run as a two-year-old and show whether or not it has inherited the fast genes of its sire and dame.

If you bought a filly, the case is rather different. There is no need to take the horse out of training when it becomes a three-year-old. She could run as a four-year-old and possibly increase her winnings. When released from training, a filly will require a nomination; this should be considered cautiously. If the match is successful, it will still be 3 to 4 years before the initial mating can be judged to be financially successful. Total runnings costs for all the horses on the flat are about five to six times total prize money.

There are several City schemes for private investors to buy a share in a racing or breeding company. Ask your broker or professional adviser for details of these.

10 USEFUL ADDRESSES

● **101   Where do I go for more information?**

1 Introduction

The Law Society
113 Chancery Lane
London WC2 (01-242 1222)

Inland Revenue
Somerset House
Strand
London WC2 (01-438 6622)

2 Saving your money

British Insurance Association
Aldemary House
Queen Street
London EC4 (01-248 4477)

Barclays Bank

Life Offices Association
Aldemary House
Queen Street
London EC4 (01-248 4477)
54 Lombard Street
London EC3 (01-623 4311)

Trustee Savings Bank
3 Copthall Avenue
London EC2 (01-588 9292)

Building Societies Association
14 Park Street
London W1 (01-629 0515)

Co-operative Bank
78 Cornhill
London EC3 (01-283 5691)

Lloyds Bank
71 Lombard Street
London EC3 (01-626 1500)

Midland Bank
Poultry and Princes Street
London EC2 (01-606 9911)

National Giro Bank
10 Milk Street
London EC2 (01-600 6020)

National Westminster Bank
41 Lothbury
London EC2 (01-606 6060)

Royal Bank of Scotland
42 St Andrews Square
Edinburgh EH2 2YE
(031 596 8555)

Clydesdale Bank
30 St Vincent Place
Glasgow G1 2HL
(041 248 7070)

Bank of Scotland
The Mound
Edinburgh RH1 1YZ
(031 221 7071)

3 National Savings

Department for National Savings
375 Kensington High Street
London W14 (01-603 2000)

Department for National Savings
Bonds and Stock Office
Preston New Road
Marten, Blackpool
Lancashire FY3 91P
(0253 66151)

4 Stocks and shares

International Stock Exchange
London EC2 (01-588 2355)

Unit Trust Association
Park House
Finsbury Circus
London EC2 (01-628 0871)

5 Other financial markets

London Futures & Options Exchange
St Katherine's Dock
London E1 9AX

London Metal Exchange
Plantation House
Fenchurch Street
London EC3 (01-626 3311)

Lloyds of London
Lime Street
London EC3 (01-623 7100)

LIFFE
Royal Exchange
London EC3 (01-623 0444)

De Beers Consolidated Mines Ltd
40 Holborn Viaduct
London EC1 (01-353 1577)

6 Property

British Property Timeshare Association
Langham House
308 Regent Street
London W1 (01-637 8049)

National House Building Council
58 Portland Place
London W1 (01-637 1248)

Royal Institute of Chartered Surveyors
12 Great George Street
London SW1 (01-222 7000)

Department of the Environment
2 Marsham Street
London SW1 (01-212 4688)

Incorporated Society of Valuers and
Auctioneers
9 Cadogan Gate
London SW1 (01-235 2282)

National Association of Estate Agents
Arbon House
21 Jury Street
Warwick CV34 4EH (0926 496800)

Forestry

Economic Forestry Group
Forestry House
Great Haseley
Oxford OX9 7PG (08446 571)

Fountain Forestry
37 Queen Anne Street
London W1M 9FB
(01-631 0485)

Farming

Strutt & Parker
13 Hill Street
London W1X 8DL
(01-629 7282)

7 Small Businesses

Small Firms Information Centres:

The national telephone number is
Freefone 'Enterprise'.

Scotland
57 Bothwell Street
Glasgow G2 6TU
(041 248 6014)

Rosebery House
Haymarket Terrace
Edinburgh EH12 5EZ
(031 337 9595)

Wales
16 St David's House
Wood Street
Cardiff CF1 1ER (0222 396116)

North
Centro House
3 Cloth Market
Central House
Newcastle upon Tyne
NE1 3EE
(0632 325353)

North West
320-325 Royal Exchange Building
St Ann's Square
Manchester M2 7AH (061 832 5282)

Yorkshire and Humberside
1 Park Row
City Square
Leeds LS1 5NR (0532 445151)

Useful Addresses

East Midlands
Severn House
20 Middle Pavement
Nottingham NG1 7DW
(0602 581205)

West Midlands
6th Floor Ladywood House
Stephenson Street
Birmingham B2 4DT
(021 643 3344)

East
Carlyle House
Carlyle Road
Cambridge CB4 3DN
(0223 63312)

London and South East
Ebury House
Ebury Bridge Road
London SW1W 8QD
(01-730 8451)

South West
5th Floor
The Pithay
Bristol BS1 2NB
(0272 294546)

A similar service is provided in Northern Ireland by the Department of Commerce

Investors in Industry
91 Waterloo Road
London SE1 (01-928 7822)

London Enterprise Agency
69 Cannon Street
London EC4 (01-236 2676)

9 Art, antiques and others

British Antique Dealers' Association
20 Rutland Gate
London SW7 1BD (01-589 4128)

The London and Provincial Antique Dealers' Association
112 Brompton Road
London SW3 (01-584 0294)

Incorporated Society of Valuers and Auctioneers
9 Cadogan Gate
London SW1X 0AS (01-235 2282)

Phillips
7 Blenheim Street
London W1 (01-629 6602)

Christie's
8 King Street
St James, London SW1 6QT
(01-539 9060)

Bonham's
Montpelier Street
London SW7 (01-584 9161)

Sotheby's
34 New Bond Street
London W1 (01-493 8080)

Coins
British Numismatic Trade Association
(Secretary, Mrs C. Deane)
P.O. Box 52C
Esher
Surrey KT10 8PW (0372 62568)

Spink & Son Ltd
King Street
London SW1 (01-930 7888)

British Association of Numismatic Societies
(Hon. Sec. K.F. Sugden)
Department of Numismatics
Manchester Museum
The University
Oxford Road
Manchester

Seaby's Coins and Medals
16 Charing Cross Road
London WC2 (01-836 0631)

Dealers
A H Baldwin & Son Ltd
11 Adelphi Terrace
London WC2 (01-930 6879)

Stanley Gibbons Currency Ltd
395 Strand
London WC2 (01-836 8444)

Lubbocks
315 Regent Street
London W1 (01-637 7922)

Cars
British Car Auctions
Expedier House
Union Road
Farnham
Surrey (0252 711222)

Wine
Wine and Spirit Educational Trust
5 King's House
Kennet Wharf Lane
Upper Thames Street
London EC4V 3AJ (01-236 3551/2)

Leading merchants include:
Justerini & Brooks
51 St James's Street
London SW1A 1LZ (01-493 8721)
and
39 George Street
Edinburgh EG2 2HN (01-226 4202)

Berry Bros & Rudd Ltd
3 St James's Street
London SW1 (01-930 1888)

Saccone & Speed Ltd
11 Cosmo Place
London WC1 (01-837 6578)

Stamps
Stanley Gibbons Ltd
399 Strand
London WC2R 0LX (01-836 8444)

Racing
The British Bloodstock Agency Ltd
11a Albermarle Street
London W1 (01-493 9402)

Racehorse Owners' Association
42 Portman Square
London W1 (01-486 6977)

The Scottish Council (Development and Industry)
1 Castle Street, Edinburgh EH2 3AJ. They also have offices in Glasgow,
Aberdeen, Inverness and London. Their aim is to promote the industrial and social
development of Scotland.

Department of Industry
The Department can give Regional Development Grants to what they call "assisted
areas". These are divided into three categories: intermediate areas, development
areas and special development areas, and the scale of the grant varies according to
which type of area you qualify for. Most assisted areas are in the North and North
West of Britain including Wales and Scotland. Write for information to the
Regional Development Grants Division, Department of Industry, Millbank,
London SW1.